MW01008615

There is perhaps no more important spiritual discipline that Christians wish they were more consistent in exercising than prayer. Many believers recognize a deficiency in their prayer lives but are at a loss to know how to make any serious progress toward consistent growth. In *Persistent Prayer,* Guy M. Richard carefully teaches on biblical prayer from both the Old and New Testaments, asking the reader practical and engaging questions. This book will encourage you to seek the God who loves to hear and answer the prayers of those who pour their hearts out before him.

—**Nick Batzig**, Associate Editor, Ligonier Ministries; Senior Pastor, Church Creek Presbyterian, Charleston

It sounds axiomatic, but God answers prayer. If for no other reason, we should pray more. Guy Richard offers to the church a clear and encouraging path to reclaim and revive prayer as the grace of pleading with God. Honestly, I don't pray as much or as earnestly as I should. I fear most would give a similar confession. Yet this book does not indict as much as it encourages. It is written not from the lofty perches of the academy but from the humble heart of one hungry to know God. When you read this book, you will find one who—like you—struggles to pray and yet rejoices to know that God graciously welcomes and answers our prayers.

—**Anthony J. Carter**, Lead Pastor, East Point Church, East Point, Georgia; Coauthor, *Dying to Speak: Meditations from the Cross*

Guy Richard's book on prayer may be small, but its impact on the heart is mighty. It not only encourages but also equips the reader to cry out to God in prayer. Be prepared: after reading this book, you'll want to pray big, God-honoring prayers.
—**Christina Fox**, Author, *A Holy Fear: Trading Lesser Fears for the Fear of the Lord*

I love this book! In an inviting and compelling way, *Persistent Prayer* captures the desperate, urgent need we have to pray. As you read through these pages, you will find yourself encouraged and inspired to talk to God. Thank you, Guy, for giving us such clear answers, anchored in the Scriptures, for why we should pray. What a gift.
—**Crawford W. Loritts Jr.**, Author; Speaker; Radio Host

Most Christians know that we should pray, that we ought to pray, that we need to pray. What we really need sometimes is a wise mentor to encourage us along the way so that we actually take up the practice of prayer. Guy Richard is such a mentor. Graciously, winsomely, compellingly, he prods us along the path of lifting our desires to our good and gracious God, knowing that he does, and will, answer our prayers for his glory. Here's a rich source of encouragement to spend time with our loving God!
—**Sean Michael Lucas**, Senior Pastor, Independent Presbyterian Church, Memphis, Tennessee; Chancellor's Professor of Church History, Reformed Theological Seminary

We don't believe in the power of prayer—we believe in the power of God, and that is why we pray. This book by Dr. Guy Richard helps us to understand what prayer is and why we pray. Having served as a faithful pastor for many years, Dr. Richard beautifully weaves together his pastoral wisdom and his academic experience to provide all Christians with a clear and accessible book to help us to grasp that prayer is more about communing with God than simply talking to God.

—**Burk Parsons**, Senior Pastor, Saint Andrews Chapel, Sanford, Florida; Editor, *Tabletalk*

PERSISTENT PRAYER

BLESSINGS OF THE FAITH

A Series

Jason Helopoulos
Series Editor

Covenantal Baptism, by Jason Helopoulos
Expository Preaching, by David Strain
Persistent Prayer, by Guy M. Richard

PERSISTENT PRAYER

GUY M. RICHARD

P&R
PUBLISHING
P.O. BOX 817 • PHILLIPSBURG • NEW JERSEY 08865-0817

If you find this book helpful, consider writing a review online
—or contact P&R at editorial@prpbooks.com with your comments.
We'd love to hear from you.

Italics within Scripture quotations indicate emphasis added.

Printed in the United States of America

Library of Congress Cataloging-in-Publication Data

Names: Richard, Guy M., author.
Title: Persistent prayer / Guy M. Richard.
Description: Phillipsburg, New Jersey : P&R Publishing, [2021] | Series: Blessings of the faith | Summary: "Informative, encouraging, and practical, this short book will serve as a helpful primer for pastors, elders, study groups, and Christians who seek encouragement and instruction on prayer and its blessings"-- Provided by publisher.
Identifiers: LCCN 2021015016 | ISBN 9781629958729 (hardcover) | ISBN 9781629958736 (epub) | ISBN 9781629958743 (mobi)
Subjects: LCSH: Prayer--Christianity.
Classification: LCC BV210.3 .R53 2021 | DDC 248.3/2--dc23
LC record available at https://lccn.loc.gov/2021015016

For Tim Murr and Al Chestnut, fellow elders in the Presbyterian Church in America and faithful brothers in Christ, who have encouraged me and set before me an example of heartfelt and heart-filled prayer. I am grateful for your influence in my life.

CONTENTS

FOREWORD

It has often been said—sometimes with a sense of humor and sometimes in annoyance—that Presbyterian and Reformed churches love to do things "decently and in order." I can understand both the humor and the frustration that lie behind that sentiment. We love our plans, our minutes, our courts, and our committees. Presbyterian and Reformed folks have been known to appoint committees just to oversee other committees (reminding me of the old *Onion* headline that announced "New Starbucks Opens in Rest Room of Existing Starbucks"). We like doing things so decently that we expect our church officers to know three things: the Bible, our confessions, and a book with *Order* in its title.

But before we shake our heads in disbelief at those uber-Reformed types (physician, heal thyself!), we should recall that before "decently and in order" was a Presbyterian predilection, it was a biblical command (see 1 Cor. 14:40). Paul's injunction for the church to be marked by propriety and decorum, to be well-ordered like troops drawn up in ranks, is a fitting conclusion to a portion of Scripture that deals with confusion regarding gender, confusion at the Lord's Table, confusion about spiritual gifts, confusion in the body of Christ, and confusion in public worship. "Decently and in order" sounds pretty good compared to the mess that prevailed in Corinth.

A typical knock on Presbyterian and Reformed Christians is that though supreme in head, they are deficient in heart. We are the emotionless stoics, the changeless wonders, God's frozen chosen. But such veiled insults would not have impressed the apostle Paul, for he knew that the opposite of order in the church is not free-flowing spontaneity; it is self-exalting chaos. God never favors confusion over peace (see 1 Cor. 14:33). He never pits theology against doxology or head against heart. David Garland put it memorably: "The Spirit of ardor is also the Spirit of order."[1]

When Jason Helopoulos approached me about writing a foreword for this series, I was happy to oblige—not only because Jason is one of my best friends (and we both root for the hapless Chicago Bears) but because these careful, balanced, and well-reasoned volumes will occupy an important place on the book stalls of Presbyterian and Reformed churches. We need short, accessible books written by thoughtful, seasoned pastors for regular members on the foundational elements of church life and ministry. That's what we need, and that's what this series delivers: wise answers to many of the church's most practical and pressing questions.

This series of books on Presbyterian and Reformed theology, worship, and polity is not a multivolume exploration of 1 Corinthians 14:40, but I am glad it is unapologetically written with Paul's command in mind. The reality is that every church will worship in some way, pray in some way, be led in some way, be structured in some way, and do baptism and the Lord's Supper in some way. Every church is living out some form of theology—even if that theology is based on pragmatism instead of biblical principles. Why wouldn't we want the life we share in the church to be shaped by the best exegetical, theological, and historical reflections? Why wouldn't we want to be thoughtful instead of thoughtless? Why wouldn't we want all things in the life we live together to be done decently and in good order? That's not the Presbyterian and Reformed way. That's God's way, and Presbyterian and Reformed Christians would do well not to forget it.

Kevin DeYoung
Senior Pastor, Christ Covenant Church
Matthews, North Carolina

Introduction

THE BLESSING OF PRAYER

Sixteen years ago, I experienced something that forced me to look at prayer and my own practice of it much more closely than I ever had before. That something was Hurricane Katrina. The destruction and upheaval it left in its wake drove me and many others around me to devote ourselves to prayer in ways that we had not previously.

In August 2005, about two months after I accepted the call to serve as pastor of First Presbyterian Church in Gulfport, Mississippi, and about two months before I planned to arrive and officially start, Hurricane Katrina destroyed the entire church facility and the homes of nearly sixty families in the congregation. Almost everyone living on the Mississippi Gulf Coast was affected by the storm: some lost their homes, some lost their businesses, some lost their churches, and some lost all three. The devastation was absolutely incredible. It will remain etched in my mind for as long as I am alive. The whole area looked like a war zone. What remained of people's homes and possessions was scattered everywhere as far as the eye could see. Huge craters were so widespread along the beachfront highway that it looked like the whole place had been carpet-bombed. Approximately thirty families in the church had nothing but a foundation left to their homes. Another thirty families had homes that were still intact but had been damaged by having anywhere from seven to seventeen feet of water in them for days on end in the sweltering summer heat.

As a not-yet-ordained recent seminary graduate, I had absolutely no idea what to do in this situation. If there was a class in seminary on how to lead a church that had experienced this kind of devastation, I had obviously missed it. I was in over my head, and I knew it.

Looking back now, I see that the whole situation was a severe mercy from the Lord in so many ways. It taught me important lessons about myself, about ministry, and about the church. But, more importantly, it drove me to pray. The elders of the church called the congregation to join us in prayer and fasting. We pleaded with the Lord to hear our prayers and to provide the wisdom, the finances, the know-how, and the peace and unity that we needed to move forward. And you know what? The Lord provided. He answered our prayers, many of them visibly for all to see. It was a high-water mark in the life of the congregation, to be sure. In many ways, it was a high-water mark in my life too.

Much of the material in this book is the fruit of those early years after the hurricane. My hope is that it will be helpful for everyone who takes it up. My hope is that it will teach us more about prayer. But what I really want is for it to encourage and motivate us to give ourselves more fully to the practice of prayer. The hurricane helped me to see what a blessing prayer is in the Christian life and how important it is for us to be praying with persistence. It is my desire that this book would do the same thing for you.

How Is Prayer a Blessing?

In the aftermath of Hurricane Katrina, God routinely answered our congregation's prayers in very visible ways. Over and over again, we had needs that we couldn't meet ourselves, and we had nowhere else to turn for help. So we prayed, frequently with great desperation, and we saw God answer time and again in ways that clearly showed us he was providing for us.

That is one of the greatest blessings of prayer. You and I get to see God work, and when we do, our faith is strengthened and our resolve to pray is increased. To be sure, God doesn't need our prayers. As the sovereign God of the universe, he is able to do all things at all times all by himself. But he stoops down to use our prayers as means to accomplish his perfect purposes. You and I, therefore, have the tremendous privilege of being coworkers with the God of the universe when we pray. And that is a blessing indeed.

Yet prayer is a blessing not only because it strengthens our faith when we see God answer and because it bestows upon us the wonderful privilege of being coworkers with God but because it gives us recourse in times of trouble. Joseph Scriven has captured this idea so beautifully in his well-known hymn "What a Friend We Have in Jesus."

> What a Friend we have in Jesus,
> all our sins and griefs to bear!
> What a privilege to carry
> everything to God in prayer!
> O what peace we often forfeit,
> O what needless pain we bear,
> all because we do not carry
> everything to God in prayer.
> Have we trials and temptations?
> Is there trouble anywhere?
> We should never be discouraged:
> take it to the Lord in prayer![1]

In the midst of the destruction caused by Hurricane Katrina, we realized anew and afresh that we had access to someone who could actually do something to help, someone who not only held all power and authority but was also altogether gracious and compassionate toward us, someone who loved us and was for us forevermore in Christ. That, too, is a tremendous blessing, and it belongs to every Christian in and through prayer.

The Importance of Prayer

Even the most mature Christians struggle with prayer from time to time. We forget the blessing it provides. We lose sight of its importance. We allow urgent things to push important things like prayer to the periphery of our lives—until a storm or a difficult providence enters our experience and reorients our priorities.

Hurricane Katrina had that effect in my life and in the lives of many of God's people who were living on the Mississippi Gulf Coast at the time. All of a sudden, our world was turned upside down. Everything was taken away. Basic necessities, like food and water, became our most pressing needs. We could no longer hop in the car and run down to the local grocery store, because we didn't have gasoline to drive (it became as precious as gold), and, even if we did, none of the stores were open anyway. All we had was prayer. It seems strange now to say that. Prayer, theologically speaking, is never a last resort for us as Christians. But, experientially, it oftentimes is such in our actual practice.

The hurricane reminded me and many others of how crucial prayer is in the Christian life. It showed us that prayer is indispensable because of what it is, because of what it does, and because of how necessary it is in the Christian life. In an effort to motivate believers to give ourselves to persistent prayer, this book will devote a chapter to discussing each of these factors. Why should we pray? I invite you to join me as we seek to answer this question together.

1

THE NATURE OF PRAYER

I love exercise. Those who know me well know that this is true. But I have come to learn through the years that my definition of what constitutes exercise is different from most people's. For me, exercise involves as much pain as possible. I enjoy the pain, or, more accurately, I enjoy the challenge of not succumbing to it and of pushing myself to go faster, harder, or farther than I thought I could. I have several close friends, however, who see what I have described as being more like torture than exercise, and because they see it this way, they cannot understand why anyone in his or her right mind would want to subject himself or herself to it on a regular basis. My friends would all acknowledge that exercise offers clear health benefits for those who take it up, but when it is understood in the way that I have defined it, they not only want no part of it themselves but even question my sanity for giving my time and energy to it.

How we define something is closely connected with our understanding of why we should (or shouldn't) do it.

This is true of exercise, and it's also true of prayer. If we think of prayer as simply having a conversation with God, then we will probably struggle more with why we should do it than if we think of it as something as essential as eating or breathing. No one has to tell us to eat or breathe. We know these activities are essential to life. I am convinced that when we understand what prayer is, we will see better why we should give ourselves to it wholeheartedly.

Finding a Definition for Prayer

The Westminster Shorter Catechism defines prayer as "an offering up of our desires unto God" and then adds several phrases that qualify what kind of "desires" we should be "offering up": "for things agreeable to his will, in the name of Christ, with confession of our sins, and thankful acknowledgement of his mercies."[1] If we take this definition at face value, we might come away thinking that prayer is merely asking God for things (it's "an offering up of our desires unto God"). But this is not at all what the authors of the Shorter Catechism intended. We know this because of the Scripture proof text that they added to support and confirm their assertion—Psalm 62:8,[2] which says, "Trust in him at all times, O people; *pour out your heart before him*; God is a refuge for us."

Of all the passages the writers of the catechism could have chosen to demonstrate that prayer is "an offering up of our desires unto God," why did they select one that speaks about pouring out the heart? Why didn't they choose Revelation 5:8, which likens "the prayers of the saints" in heaven to "golden bowls full of incense"? That would certainly seem to capture the idea of prayer as an "offering" better than Psalm 62:8 does. Why not John 16:23–24, Philippians 4:6, or 1 John 5:15—all of which refer to prayer in terms of requests that we present to God? These passages would also seem to do a better job at proving that prayer is "an offering up of our desires unto God." Why Psalm 62:8?

I believe the divines chose Psalm 62:8 because they were thinking of prayer as something more than simply making requests to God. This proof text tells us that the authors of the Shorter Catechism regarded prayer primarily as "pour[ing] out [our] heart[s] before [God]." The word that has frequently been used to communicate this idea is the word *pleading*.[3] We plead with God in prayer when we pour out our hearts before him. We earnestly implore him to hear us and to answer from heaven. We do this not just with our words but also with all of our heart, soul, mind, and strength. That is what the authors of the Shorter Catechism meant when they defined prayer as an "offering up of our desires unto God." The selection of the proof text tells us as much.

The Psalms frequently speak of prayer in similar terms. Thus we read that the psalmists "cry" out to the Lord, "lift up [their] soul" to him, "call upon" him, and "plead" with him for mercy and grace (see Pss. 17; 86;

102; 142—all of which are explicitly titled prayers). Moreover, they often use the words *prayer* and *plea* in parallel, thereby indicating a great deal of overlap if not outright synonymy (see Pss. 6:9; 86:6; 142:1–2; 143:1). Even when the psalmists are not explicitly praying, they still address the Lord in ways that reflect a pouring out of their hearts before him. Here I am thinking particularly of passages like Psalm 9:1–2, in which David pours out his heart in praise and thanksgiving to the Lord:

> I will give thanks to the Lord with my whole heart;
> I will recount all of your wonderful deeds.
> I will be glad and exult in you;
> I will sing praise to your name, O Most High.

Besides these psalms, other passages in Scripture suggest that prayer is a whole-souled pleading with the Lord. Hannah, in 1 Samuel 1, is described as "pouring out [her] soul before the Lord" (v. 15). Solomon, in his prayer of dedication for the newly built temple, routinely uses the words *prayer* and *plea* interchangeably (see 1 Kings 8:28, 30, 33, 38, 44–45, 47–49, 54). In the New Testament, moreover, we see prayer presented as "heart pleading" in passages like Matthew 9:38, Luke 22:31–32, and Acts 4:31—all of which use a word for prayer (*deomai* in the Greek) that is most frequently translated "beg" or "implore" and that, in most cases, explicitly involves an earnestness that comes from the heart.[4]

The most obvious support in the New Testament for seeing prayer as pleading, however, comes from Jesus's teaching on prayer in Luke 11:5–10. In this passage, Jesus gives an example of a man who has no food to set before a friend who is visiting from out of town. Even though it is midnight, the man ventures out to try to borrow some food for his friend.[5] Driven by desperation, he doesn't simply "offer up his desires" in a clinical fashion. He doesn't just nonchalantly ask his neighbor for food; he asks, and he seeks, and he knocks, and he keeps on persisting until he receives what he so desperately needs (in verses 9–10, note the present tense is used in each case, showing continuous action). Thus Jesus teaches us that prayer is pleading that is motivated by a need that we cannot meet ourselves and that we desperately want God to supply for us. It is this kind of heartfelt and heart-filled prayer that Jesus says will be answered by the Lord (vv. 8–10)—a subject that we will take up in the next chapter.

Prayer Is Heart Work

If prayer involves pouring out our hearts to God, then we can see immediately why we should be engaging in it. We should do so precisely *because* it involves our hearts. The Bible everywhere teaches us that God is concerned chiefly about matters of the heart (see Gen. 6:5; 1 Sam. 16:7; Matt. 6:21; 12:34; Acts 15:8). This is especially true in regard to the Christian life. We not only are told that the "great and first commandment" is to love the Lord our God with all our hearts (Matt. 22:37–38) but also see that if we do anything in the Christian life without engaging our hearts, then we do it "in vain" and are guilty of the same kind of hypocrisy that Jesus accused the Pharisees and scribes of in Matthew 15:7–9.

To say that prayer is pleading is, therefore, simply to say that it is an expression of the Christian life. When we pray, we engage in heart work: we commune with the Lord, and we experience real intimacy with the God of the universe. No doubt this is the primary reason why our Lord and Savior spent so much time in prayer during the course of his earthly ministry. It wasn't because he had so many requests to present to God. It was because he was engaging in heart work with his heavenly Father, enjoying extended seasons of intimate communion with him. That is precisely what prayer is meant to be for us too.

Prayer Is Relationship Glue

As a pastor, I have had the privilege of doing quite a bit of marriage counseling over the years. In every situation in which a couple has come to me for help, I have found that there has been almost no intimacy between them for some time leading up to their visit. And they are surprised that they are having trouble! Intimacy in marriage is like relationship glue. It holds couples together. It gives us more bandwidth to handle the conflict and disagreement that inevitably arise.

Prayer is like that in the Christian life. It is relationship glue. It bonds our hearts more and more to the Lord and holds us to him more firmly. The Scottish Puritan Samuel Rutherford once said that when we pray, our faith kisses Christ, and he kisses our soul.[6] Even though we may shy away from that kind of language today, we would do well to hear Rutherford's point, which is that prayer is intimacy with Christ. No doubt that is one reason why so many in the Reformed community have called prayer a means of grace. When it is done rightly, it strengthens the relationship between the Christian and the Lord Jesus Christ.

This view of prayer is further confirmed by Paul's words in 1 Corinthians 7:5, where the apostle exhorts married couples to "not deprive one another, except perhaps by agreement for a limited time, that you may devote yourselves to prayer." According to Paul, only one thing should keep a husband and wife from pursuing intimacy with each other, and that is pursuing intimacy with God in prayer. Given the priority of our relationship with God over every other relationship (see Matt. 22:37–39) and the fact that prayer involves pouring out our hearts to the Lord, we would expect Paul to say this; and he does. The intimacy of prayer is even more important than the intimacy of marriage.

Prayer Involves a Sense of Our Need

Just as the man's need for food in Luke 11:5–10 drove him to ask, seek, and knock, so our own needs should lead us to do the same. Without a sense of need, we tend to pray in a more clinical fashion. We don't pour out our hearts before the Lord, because we aren't *really* convinced that we must have what we are praying for. But when we find ourselves in trouble, when hardship or disaster comes into our lives, then we typically plead with the Lord with great fervency, because then we understand that we have a real need that we cannot meet ourselves.

Part of the reason we struggle to sense need in our lives could be that many of us are not stepping out in faith and taking risks for the Lord. I know that is often true for me, anyway. The more I take on ministry projects and opportunities that are beyond my capacities and resources, the more I am forced to pray and to lean on God for help. The more I step out in faith and attempt big things for the Lord, the more I am compelled to plead with him in prayer because I know that I am doomed to fail without it.

After Hurricane Katrina, I quickly realized that our church had to start some kind of a rebuilding ministry to help our own members and then the community at large to get back into their homes. We lacked not only the construction know-how for this kind of project but also the funding for it. We knew that we needed the Lord to provide in a big way, and our need forced us to do more than just ask; it forced us to pour out our hearts before the Lord and to plead with him earnestly for his help.

Prayer May Also Require Preparation

Because prayer entails pouring out our hearts to God, we may have to prepare our hearts before we pray. Sometimes our circumstances provide all the preparation that is necessary. When someone we love is hanging on to life by a thread or when we lose our jobs and are struggling to make ends meet, we probably won't require much else to prepare us to pour out our hearts. In seasons like these, we are all too aware of our need for the Lord to intervene and are desperate for him to do so. But when our days are more pleasant and we are not as aware of our need, we find it hard to pour out our hearts. If we don't prepare ourselves first, we go cold before the Lord and our prayers most likely reflect that coldness. This may be one reason why so many of us yawn or fall asleep in the middle of our prayers. We haven't prepared our hearts beforehand.

In my own experience, it feels like a thin layer of ice forms over my heart overnight. I have to break that thin layer each day before I can spend time with the Lord in prayer. To do this, I have found that I must meditate deeply on a particular passage of Scripture or read or listen to something that rouses my heart and reminds me of what I am about to do. I have also been helped by pausing for a few moments before I pray to remind myself that I am walking into the presence of the God of the universe who loves me and gave his Son for me.

Heart preparation is especially important for those who pray regularly in the presence of others. Richard Baxter exhorts those who preach, teach, or pray in front of others (which, by the way, is something most of us will do at some point in our lives) to labor to awaken our own hearts beforehand, because if we don't, the coldness of our own hearts will be reflected in the hearts of our hearers. Baxter encourages us to "read some rousing, awakening book, or meditate on the weight of the subject of which you are to speak, and on the great necessity of your people's souls" so that everyone may be warmed by the fire that is thereby rekindled in our hearts.[7]

Pleading Our Case

If prayer really does involve pouring out our hearts before God in a way that is motivated by an awareness of our need, then this means that our prayers will, therefore, also seek to be as persuasive as possible. I don't mean to suggest that we try to twist God's arm into doing something that he originally didn't want to do—as if that could happen. But if we are really pouring out our hearts to God, we will want to be as persuasive as possible, won't we? As we plead with the Lord, we will, like good attorneys, plead our case before him.

This is what Abraham does in Genesis 18:22–33, when he intercedes on behalf of Sodom. He makes like a good attorney and argues his case before the Lord. His argument, which is predicated upon the Lord's justice, is that it is not right for God "to put the righteous to death with the wicked" (v. 25). Abraham pushes this argument until God agrees not to destroy unrighteous Sodom if only ten righteous persons are found in the city.

Moses does something similar in Exodus 32:11–14, after the incident with the golden calf. He "implore[s] the LORD his God" (v. 11) to be merciful toward the people of Israel, and his plea is expressed by way of two arguments. First, Moses argues that if God destroys the people of Israel, the Egyptians will have grounds to impugn his character. They will say, "With evil intent did he bring [the people] out, to kill them in the mountains and to consume them from the face of the earth" (v. 12). Second, Moses argues that because God "swore by [his] own self, and said to [Abraham, Isaac, and Jacob], 'I will multiply your offspring as the stars of heaven, and all this land that I have promised I will give to your offspring, and they shall inherit it forever' " (v. 13), he must, therefore, be merciful to the Israelites and not destroy them.

David does the same thing in Psalm 30:8–10, among other places. He bases his "plea" for God to be merciful to him on the argument that God will gain more glory from his life than from his death:

To you, O Lord, I cry,
  and to the Lord I plead for mercy:
"What profit is there in my death,
  if I go down to the pit?
Will the dust praise you?
  Will it tell of your faithfulness?
Hear, O Lord, and be merciful to me!
  O Lord, be my helper!"

But Jehoshaphat may provide the best example of all in the great prayer that he offers in 2 Chronicles 20:5–12. With the Moabites, Ammonites, and Meunites on his doorstep preparing to make war with the people of God (vv. 1–2), Jehoshaphat declares a fast throughout the land of Judah, enters the house of the Lord, and prays. His prayer is organized around three main questions: "Are you not . . . ?" (v. 6), "Did you not . . . ?" (vv. 7–11), and "Will you not . . . ?" (v. 12). Jehoshaphat's plea for mercy begins with his rehearsing the very character of God: Are you not the sovereign God of the universe, the one who is able to do as you please such that "none is able to withstand you" (v. 6)? Jehoshaphat then recounts the ways that God has worked in the past to bring salvation for his people and to fight for them. He concludes by appealing to God to do it again in this present crisis with the Moabites, Ammonites, and Meunites. Finally, Jehoshaphat acknowledges that God may or may not heed his argument and may or may not answer his prayer. He prays, and he waits to see what God will do: "We do not know what to do, but our eyes are on you" (v. 12).

Making an argument to the Lord isn't going to twist God's arm, and it isn't going to give him information that he overlooked or was unaware of until you or I offered it to him in prayer. What it *does* do, however, is force us to think through what we are praying for and why. It forces us to think about why God would answer our prayers in the first place, thus aligning us more with his character and will. In other words, praying this way changes us. It helps us to "think God's thoughts after Him."[8] It helps to make his will and his desires become ours.

A good example of this can be seen in the life of Moses. After making his argument with the Lord in Exodus 32:11–14, Moses later intercedes for the people again and even prays that God would punish him instead of the people of Israel: "But now, if you will forgive their sin—but if not, please blot me out of your book that you have written" (v. 32). Even though the Lord explicitly tells us that it is not his will to pardon the people who sinned against him (see vv. 33–34)—and, thus, we might wonder how Moses's pleading has changed him to "think God's thoughts after Him"—it is nonetheless true that Moses has been changed. His pleading has at least aligned him more with the character of God, because he exhibits in verse 32 the very character that we see on display explicitly in Exodus 34:6, where the Lord refers to himself as "a God merciful and gracious, slow to anger, and abounding in steadfast love and faithfulness."

When we look at Abraham's, Moses's, and David's arguments, we see their desire for the glory of God and their compassion for others. Abraham is concerned not only about how God's justice will be perceived but also about what will happen to the hundreds or thousands of people in the city of Sodom. Moses is concerned about God's reputation among the Egyptians, but he also desires to see many lives saved among his own people. And David is interested not only in God's glory but also in other people seeing that glory. Thus we conclude that it is not enough simply to make an argument; we must make an argument *that will hold weight with the Lord* because it is in keeping with his character and his revealed will. And when we pray this way over time, we become like what we pray for.

Could it be that one of the reasons why so many of us and so many of our churches have become more inward facing is that our prayers have become more and more preoccupied with ourselves and the circumstances of our own lives and ministries? Praying according to the character and will of God produces Christians who are more attuned to his character and will in all areas of their lives. Kingdom praying really does produce kingdom Christians. That is one reason why we should pray—and why we should make an argument that carries weight with God when we do.

Pleading and Praise Go Together

Praise is an important part of prayer. I would even go so far as to say that it is the *most* important part. Because all prayer is Godward, it rightly takes into account who we are praying to and what he is due. Thus, when Jesus teaches his disciples to pray, he begins with praise and adoration (see Luke 11:2). And we can't get very far through the Psalms before we see the same overwhelming emphasis. Does this emphasis on adoration, however, contradict our definition of prayer as pleading?

I readily acknowledge that some readers may hear me saying "supplication" when I define prayer in terms of "pleading." But, if you remember, that is not the way I am using the word. When I speak of prayer as pleading, I am simply referring to the fact that it is "pour[ing] out your heart" to the Lord (Ps. 62:8). Seen in this way, pleading necessarily entails heart work, and heart work is fundamental to ascribing praise to the Lord. God is not looking for us to offer praise and adoration with our lips while our hearts are far from him (see Isa. 29:13; Matt. 15:8). Rather, as we have said, he is looking for us to pour out our hearts before him. We can do this in praise and adoration because we see God as glorious and long to acknowledge it in his presence. What is more, we can plead with the Lord to increase our awareness of and our love for his praiseworthiness and to pour out his Spirit on the nations so that many people come to see him who is worthy of praise and adoration. This in and of itself brings glory to God.

Remember, too, that pleading necessarily involves making an argument consistent with the character and will of God. If we make this kind of an argument, we can see the connection Scripture teaches between pleading and praising. We extol the Lord for who he is and for what he has done, and we use that as a basis for petitioning him to help us in our present circumstances. That is how Solomon prays in 1 Kings 8 (see vv. 15, 23–30, 56–59). It is also Jehoshaphat's pattern of prayer in 2 Chronicles 20, and it is how David prays in Psalm 9.

What about Confession and Thanksgiving?

The well-known acrostic ACTS includes confession and thanksgiving alongside adoration and supplication. When we define prayer as pleading or as a pouring out of our hearts, we can more readily see that confession and thanksgiving—like praise and adoration—are not meant to be clinically detached endeavors that are engaged in rotely. God wants confession that proceeds from hearts deeply grieved over our sin and its impact in our lives and the lives of the people around us. That is certainly the idea in Psalm 51, where David pours out his heart to the Lord in confession of sin. From the very beginning of this great psalm, David pleads with the Lord—"Have mercy on me, O God"—and demonstrates his "broken and contrite heart" (v. 17) in the language that he uses throughout:

> For I know my transgressions,
> and my sin is ever before me.
> Against you, you only, have I sinned
> and done what is evil in your sight,
> so that you may be justified in your words
> and blameless in your judgment. (vv. 3–4)

> Cast me not away from your presence,
> and take not your Holy Spirit from me.
> Restore to me the joy of your salvation. (vv. 11–12)

> Deliver me from bloodguiltiness, O God,
> O God of my salvation. (v. 14)

> A broken and contrite heart, O God, you will not
> despise. (v. 17)

Such language drips with pathos. It is hard to imagine David praying these words with anything even remotely approaching clinical detachment or half-hearted interest.

In the same way, thanksgiving involves more than simply uttering the words "thank you." It overflows from a heart that is filled with joy and gratitude for what the Lord has done. It may not always manifest itself as it does in the case of the leper who returned to show appreciation for being made well—he returned "praising God with a loud voice; and he fell on his face at Jesus' feet, giving him thanks" (Luke 17:15–16). But it will always involve a pouring out of the heart before the Lord.

Second, defining prayer as pleading or a pouring out of the heart helps us to see that our confession and thanksgiving ought to be specific. Rather than confessing our sins very generally to the Lord, we take the details of our transgressions, lay them before him, and plead with him for forgiveness because of who he is and what he has done. The more general our confession, the less likely it is to come from the heart. When we confess our sin in detail, we feel the weight of our guilt and the corresponding glory of our forgiveness in Christ Jesus. And when we express our gratitude in detail, we show a depth of gratitude that cannot be fully conveyed in the words *thank you*.

Giving God No Rest

Prayer that pours out the heart to the Lord is not only persuasive but also persistent. What would it tell us if the man in Luke 11 asked his neighbor for food, then immediately returned home after the neighbor's initial rejection (see v. 7)? Wouldn't it tell us that the man didn't really need the food after all? If he had genuinely needed the food, wouldn't he have continued knocking and asking until he received it, no matter how long it took?

Jesus says that we ought to "ask," "seek," and "knock" when we pray (Luke 11:9–10), and he doesn't mean that we are to do each of these things only once. He uses the present-tense imperative each time, which, in Greek, shows ongoing action. This means that Jesus is telling us not to ask, seek, and knock once but to do so continually. He is saying, "Ask and keep on asking," "Seek and keep on seeking," and "Knock and keep on knocking." He wants us to persist in praying. Like Jacob, we are to hold on and not let go until and unless the Lord blesses us (see Gen. 32:26). We are to "give [God] no rest until he establishes Jerusalem and makes it a praise in the earth" (Isa. 62:7).

Bringing It All Together

Knowing that prayer is pleading, or a pouring out of our hearts to God, helps us to see why we should give our time and attention to it. Prayer is relationship glue. When we pray, we experience real intimacy with the Lord and strengthen our relationship with him. Prayer assumes that we have genuine heartfelt needs and that we really need God's help. Prayer calls us to step out in faith and take risks for the Lord, which forces us to pray bigger prayers and to be more dependent on him in our praying. As we see God working in and through us and providing for us, we are encouraged and motivated to step out in faith again. Prayer aligns us more with the character and will of God and calls us to "give him no rest" until he hears from heaven and answers us.

Questions for Further Reflection

1. What is prayer? How is the definition of prayer presented in this chapter different from what you may have thought or heard previously?
2. How does your definition of prayer affect how you pray?
3. How is prayer "relationship glue"? Do you find this idea helpful in your own Christian experience? Why or why not?
4. What are some ways to prepare your heart for prayer? How might preparation change your prayer life?
5. Have you ever "made an argument" with the Lord in prayer? What are the advantages of doing so? What might you need to watch out for when you do?
6. How is persistence in prayer connected to prayer as pleading or pouring out the heart? Why is this connection significant practically?

2

PRAYER WORKS

According to Lottery USA, the odds of winning the Mega Millions lottery are approximately 1 in 302 million.[1] At these odds, you and I are more likely to be struck by lightning multiple times, which is just one reason why I have never played the lottery myself. It feels too much like throwing money down the drain. But what if I told you about a new sweepstakes that offered a one-out-of-one or even a one-out-of-four chance of winning? Leaving aside other objections to gambling in general, my guess is that almost all of us would be interested in buying tickets with these kinds of favorable odds.

The title of this chapter may give the impression that I am speaking of prayer as a kind of new sweepstakes with one-out-of-one or one-out-of-four odds of winning. If prayer works to the degree that we always or nearly always get what we ask for, then surely we would all be interested in praying more than we do currently. If that were the case, however, it wouldn't be necessary for me to write a book answering the question "Why should we pray?" because we would all be praying as much as we possibly could already.

Almost every time I have preached on the topic of prayer, someone from the congregation has come up to me afterward with a question about unanswered prayer. Not too long ago, I was approached by a man whose wife had died a few years earlier. He told me that for months on end he had prayed earnestly to the Lord, pouring out his heart, begging for his wife to be restored to health—but to no avail. To borrow the language that Jesus uses in Luke 11:9–10, this man had "asked" but not "received," "sought" but not "found," and "knocked" but not had the door "opened" to him. In his experience, prayer hadn't worked at all—and most of us have had times in our lives when we've felt exactly the same way.

Does prayer actually work? And, if so, how? What can we say in regard to the problem of unanswered prayer? What counsel can we impart to help those who may be struggling with great hardship, like the man who lost his wife despite the fact that he had been pouring out his heart to the Lord? Those are the questions that we will take up in this chapter.

Does Prayer Actually Work?

The overwhelming testimony of Scripture is that prayer does, in fact, work. In James 4:2, for instance, the apostle directly attributes the lack his readers are experiencing in their lives to their prayerlessness: "You do not have, because you do not ask." The answer, James says, is not to murder in order to obtain what you want, nor is it to fight and quarrel until you get your way. The answer is to pray, because prayer works.

Elsewhere in his epistle, James also says, "If any of you lacks wisdom, *let him ask God,* who gives generously to all without reproach, *and it will be given him*" (James 1:5). Later on, the apostle adds that the "prayer of a righteous person has great power as it is working" (5:16). And in the next two verses, he cites the example of Elijah, who prayed that it would not rain for three and a half years. After that time had lapsed, Elijah prayed that it would rain again. Both prayers were demonstrably answered by the Lord.

Jesus, too, says similar things on many occasions in the Gospels. In John 14:14, for instance, he instructs his disciples to ask for anything in his name, and he will do it for them. In John 15:16 and 16:23, Jesus tells his disciples that his heavenly Father will do anything that they ask in his name. In Matthew 18:19, he states that when any two of them are in agreement, and they ask in prayer, then the Father will grant them their request. In Matthew 21:22, Jesus goes so far as to say that anyone who has faith and asks will receive whatever he or she has requested. And, last but certainly not least, Jesus proclaims that *everyone* who asks receives, *everyone* who seeks finds, and *everyone* who knocks has the door opened to him or her (see Luke

11:9–10). Jesus obviously believes that prayer works, and he wants all of us who follow after him to believe it too.

But What about the Bible's Conditions and Qualifications for Prayer?

Many of the passages that I have cited on the effectiveness of prayer, however, also come with conditions and qualifications. James warns his readers that they cannot ask for anything they want and expect to receive it. They cannot "ask wrongly"—"to spend it on [their] passions" (4:3)—and still expect to get what they ask for. Similarly, Jesus qualifies his statements by adding that his disciples must ask "in his name" or must "abide" in him and have his "words abide" in them (John 15:7).

These passages, and many others, indicate that we ought not expect God to answer every prayer we make regardless of what we ask for or why. According to the Bible, several factors will at least limit the likelihood of God answering our prayers. We will examine four of these factors in more detail: not praying in the name of Jesus, not praying according to God's will, praying selfishly, and praying in the midst of persistent and unrepentant sin.

In the Name of Jesus

On several occasions Jesus tells his disciples that they will receive what they ask for if and when they pray "in his name." But what does it mean to pray in Jesus's name?

For us, names convey personal preferences or perhaps family connections. We choose names because we like them or because they have been in our families for generations. But in the Jewish culture of the Old Testament and of Jesus's day, names carried a greater significance. They tended to communicate character or work. For example, Abraham's name means "father of a multitude," and he is given this name by the Lord himself precisely because he will become "the father of a multitude of nations" (Gen. 17:5). Jacob's name means "he deceives" (see Gen. 25:26)—a moniker that describes Jacob's character and deeds for the early years of his life. But in Genesis 32, the Lord changes Jacob's name to Israel, which means "he struggles with God" (see v. 28). This new designation, which is given not only to him but to the entire nation that would come from him, describes not only Jacob's life but the life of all God's people.[2] Finally, the name of our Lord and Savior, *Jesus,* is the Greek form of the Hebrew word *Joshua,* which means "God saves."[3] He is called this precisely because he will "save his people from their sins" (Matt. 1:21). His name points us to his character (who he is) and to his work (what he will do).

To pray "in Jesus's name," therefore, is not simply to attach three words to the end of our prayers but to pray according to Jesus's character and work. This affects both *what* we pray for and *how* we pray for those things. To pray in Jesus's name is to pray for things that are in keeping with who Jesus is and what he came to do and to pray for those things in a manner that is itself consistent with Jesus's character and work.

This means, first, that we pray as those who have access to God through the blood of Jesus. We can walk boldly into the presence of God and know that we have a right to be there because of what Jesus has done on our behalf (see Heb. 4:16). We don't need to be timid or bashful in our requests or to hold back or limit our petitions. We can ask confidently, and we can make massive requests, because we know that God is—and will always be—*for* us in Christ (see Rom. 8:31).

Second, praying in Jesus's name means that we pray in the hope that God will answer us because of what Jesus has done for us. In other words, we are pleading that the blood of Christ that renders our persons acceptable to God for eternity will also render our prayers acceptable as we offer them. When we add the phrase "in Jesus's name" to the end of our prayers, we are pleading with God to hear our prayers and to answer us for Jesus's sake.

Third, praying in Jesus's name means that we pray for things that are in keeping with the work of Christ. This most obviously includes requests such as praying for unbelievers to come to faith in Christ, for the Lord to finish the work he has started within us and others, and for the boundaries of his kingdom to expand everywhere around the world. But it also includes praying for the Lord to return quickly in glory and power, for Satan's kingdom to be destroyed, and for the enemies of Christ to be vanquished once and for all.

When we do not pray in Jesus's name, we have no reason to expect that God will answer our prayers. But when we do pray in Jesus's name, according to his character and work, we have every reason to expect that God will answer. Just *how* he will answer our prayers, however, remains to be seen.

According to God's Will

The apostle John adds a familiar qualifier to prayer in 1 John 5:14–15: "This is the confidence that we have toward [God], that if we ask anything *according to his will* he hears us. And if we know that he hears us in whatever we ask, we know that we have the requests that we have asked of him." Thus, according to John, we can be confident that God will hear and answer our prayers and grant our requests only if we ask for things that are "according to his will." But what does praying according to God's will involve?

First, it involves our prayers aligning with what God wants to do. He is the sovereign Lord of all, and he always does as he pleases. Our prayers do not change God's mind or give him information that he had previously overlooked. He is all-knowing, all-wise, and altogether good. He knows what is best in every situation out of every possible contingency. Our confidence in regard to seeing our prayers answered, therefore, ultimately applies only to those things that are in accord with what God wants to happen.

When we pray "according to God's will," therefore, we say something similar to what Jesus said when he prayed in the garden of Gethsemane: "Nevertheless, not as I will, but as you will" (Matt. 26:39). In this sense, praying "according to God's will" shows faithful submission to the will of the Lord in all our requests. It is a way of acknowledging that his will is best, even if we may not know or see how.

Second, praying according to God's will involves praying scriptural prayers, because the Bible is the place where God has revealed his will to us. To borrow the language of Deuteronomy 29:29, the "secret things belong to the LORD," and we cannot know them, but "the things that are revealed belong to us and to our children forever." Prayer that is according to the will of God is thus saturated with the language of Scripture (the revealed will of God) and conducted according to the manner laid out in Scripture; and it makes requests that are in keeping with what has been revealed to us there.

When we fail to pray according to Scripture and for things that are in keeping with what it says, we, again, have no reason to expect that God will answer our prayers. But when we ask for things that are in keeping with what the Bible teaches, we have, according to John, every reason to expect that God will answer. The *way* he answers, however, may not always be what we envision.

This actually tells us a great deal about the nature of prayer. Rather than seeing it as a means of getting God to give attention to our wants or to bring him in line with our desires, we should see it as a means by which God gets our wants and desires in line with his. If the Bible is, as the Puritans used to say, the workshop of the Holy Spirit, then prayer that is according to God's will is a means that God uses to rub off the sharp edges and smooth over the rough places. It molds our desires to be more like his desires and our will to be more like his will.

Selfish Motives and Desires

James 4:3 warns us against asking "wrongly, to spend it on [our] passions." The apostle's point is that we cannot ask God for $10 million to make our lives more comfortable and expect that he will give it to us. Prayer works, but it is not a guarantee that we will receive any and every desire we have. The issue here is not so much with *what* we ask for as with *why* we are asking for it. Asking God for $10 million may well be a perfectly appropriate prayer to make. It all depends on the motives behind our request and how we intend to use the money.

The nineteenth-century English minister George Müller asked the Lord for the equivalent of $10 million and more—not all at once, mind you, but over the course of his sixty-three-year ministry—and he received what he asked for in answer to his prayers. But Müller didn't ask for this money for himself, "to spend it on [his] passions." He asked for it to fund the operation of the orphanage that he founded and directed, an orphanage that looked after almost ten thousand children in his lifetime. He asked for the money to further the work of the Lord in the world and to give God glory in and through such visible answers to his prayers.

In other words, Müller's asking for millions of dollars illustrates the words of Psalm 37:4, which says, "Delight yourself in the LORD, and he will give you the desires of your heart." It illustrates Jesus's words in John 15:7: "If you abide in me, and my words abide in you, ask whatever you wish, and it will be done for you." Müller did not ask "wrongly, to spend it on [his] passions." He asked boldly and confidently, to be sure. But his prayers came from a heart that delighted in the Lord and in his Word and sought to point to God rather than to himself.

If we delight ourselves in the Lord, if we abide in Christ and in his Word, then the way we pray and what we pray for will be affected. We will be far more concerned about God's glory and purposes than about our own. We will be far more concerned about people seeing how glorious he is than about others seeing how glorious we are. We will want him to use us for his gain far more than we want to use him for ours. If we pray this way, we will have every reason to expect that our prayers will be answered; and if we don't, we won't.

Persistent and Unrepentant Sin

Several passages in the Bible indicate that sin prevents our prayers from being answered. I am thinking especially of passages like Jeremiah 11:14–15: "I will not listen when [my people] call to me in the time of their trouble. What right has my beloved in my house, when she has done many vile deeds?" Or Isaiah 1:15–17, in which the Lord says,

> When you spread out your hands,
> I will hide my eyes from you;
> even though you make many prayers,
> I will not listen;
> your hands are full of blood.
> Wash yourselves; make yourselves clean;
> remove the evil of your deeds from before my eyes;
> cease to do evil,
> learn to do good;
> seek justice,
> correct oppression;
> bring justice to the fatherless,
> plead the widow's cause.

Proverbs 28:9 tells us that the prayer of the one who "turns away his ear from hearing the law . . . is an abomination" to the Lord. And Proverbs 15:29 states that the Lord is "far from the wicked, but he hears the prayer of the righteous," which certainly implies that sin hinders our prayers and keeps them from being answered.[4]

What do we do with passages like this? Does sin really prevent our prayers from being answered? If we have to be perfect for prayer to work, then none of our prayers would ever be answered. What is more, the Bible would contradict itself because it would be telling us both that God answers prayer and that he doesn't answer prayer (because none of us will ever be perfect until we get to heaven). So what are the abovementioned passages saying? Quite simply, the point they are teaching is that we cannot live in persistent, unrepentant sin and expect God to answer our prayers. Look at Psalm 66:18–19:

> If I had cherished iniquity in my heart,
> the Lord would not have listened.
> But truly God has listened;
> he has attended to the voice of my prayer.

The key word in these verses is "cherished." The psalmist isn't talking about committing iniquity in his heart or actions. He is talking about loving iniquity, befriending it, welcoming it into his life, and safeguarding it for a sustained period of time. He is talking about giving one's heart over to sin willfully and living in open and unrepentant rebellion against the Lord. If we do this, we have absolutely no right to expect God will listen to us and answer our prayers. God is undeniably gracious and merciful, "slow to anger and abounding in steadfast love" (Ps. 103:8). He may well answer the prayers of the one who is engaged in open rebellion against him. That is his decision. But we have no grounds to expect that he will do so.

Be Careful Not to Overqualify

These four factors tell us we cannot presume that the Lord will grant us anything just because we have asked for it. There are important qualifications to remember. But I do find it interesting that the Bible nowhere gives a comprehensive statement on prayer that dots every *i* and crosses every *t*. Oftentimes only one qualification is given in Scripture alongside the promise that God answers prayer. In James 4:2–3, for instance, James lists the single stipulation that we are not to ask "wrongly, to spend it on [our] passions." He doesn't say anything about asking according to God's will, asking in Jesus's name, or keeping ourselves from "cherishing" sin in our hearts. Similarly, when Jesus tells his disciples that God will give them whatever they ask for "in his name," he doesn't mention any other qualifications or conditions for answered prayer. He mentions only the one.

Sometimes no qualifications or conditions are given at all in the Bible, as in Jesus's teaching on prayer in Luke 11:9–10. Here, Jesus seems perfectly willing to leave his incredible statement that "everyone who asks receives, and the one who seeks finds, and to the one who knocks it will be opened" hanging in the air without any kind of qualification whatsoever. I find that fascinating. The only perfect theologian who ever walked the face of the earth did not feel the need to state his theology exhaustively or to speak with pinpoint precision on every occasion.

My question is, Why? Why would Jesus not give a thorough theological treatment of prayer? Why would he—and the apostles—be so willing on so many occasions to speak of answered prayer with only one qualification and in some cases none? The most likely answer is that if Jesus had given us a thorough treatment of prayer with all the possible qualifications and conditions, we wouldn't see the power of prayer. If James had said, "Prayer works, but not when it is done this way, or this way, or this way, or any of these other ten ways," we would lose sight of the power of prayer in the midst of all the qualifications. Jesus and his apostles wanted us to feel the weight of the promise that prayer works.

The Lord knows that some of us tend so much to theological precision that we lose sight of the power of prayer. While we must remember the qualifications that are given in Scripture, we should also be careful not to overqualify statements like the one in James 4:2 to the point where we no longer feel the weight of the truth of the matter for ourselves: we do not have because we do not ask. Why should we pray? The simple answer is because prayer works. And that gives us real motivation to do it.

How Does Prayer Work?

Prayer works, but it doesn't always work in the exact way that we envision. God is a perfect Father. He knows what we need better than we do. And while he answers our prayers, he doesn't always answer them by giving us precisely what we ask for. This is what Jesus has in mind in Luke 11, when he follows his rather surprising comment about how "everyone who asks receives" with an analogy describing how our heavenly Father provides for the needs of his children:

> What father among you, if his son asks for a fish, will instead of a fish give him a serpent; or if he asks for an egg, will give him a scorpion? (vv. 11–12)

Notice what Jesus *doesn't* say here. He doesn't say, "What father among you, if his son asks for a fish, will *always* give him a fish; or if he asks for an egg, will *always* give him an egg?" Jesus doesn't say that, because he knows every good father and mother will occasionally deny their children what they ask for. We may allow our children candy on occasion, for example, but we—who are older and wiser—know they cannot have candy all the time. We know they need a well-balanced diet, and sweets are a special treat, not a substitute for proper food. No good parent will always give his or her children exactly what they ask for every time they ask for it. And God is the same way.

But what Jesus *does* say in these verses is that when our children ask for fish, we *won't* give them serpents, and when they ask for eggs, we *won't* give them scorpions. We may not always give them fish or eggs, but we won't give them harmful things. And even though Jesus doesn't explicitly say so, his point certainly seems to be that this also applies to God in all his dealings with his children. He may not always give us exactly what we ask for, but he will never give us things that will harm us.

This, in and of itself, is a tremendous encouragement for us to pray. We know that however God chooses to answer our prayers, he will always do so in a way that is for our good. He may not give us a fish when we ask for a fish, but he will never give us a serpent or a scorpion instead.

But Jesus says more than this. He says that God will give us the "Holy Spirit" in answer to our prayers: "If you then, who are evil, know how to give good gifts to your children, how much more will the heavenly Father give the Holy Spirit to those who ask him!" (v. 13). This is not what we would expect him to say. Given the way he started his analogy, we would expect him to say that God will give "good gifts" to his children in the same way that earthly parents do to their children. That is what Jesus says in the parallel passage on prayer in Matthew 7: "If you then, who are evil, know how to give good gifts to your children, how much more will your Father who is in heaven give good things to those who ask him!" (v. 11).

But in Luke 11, he says that the Father will give us the "Holy Spirit."

Because we believe that the Bible cannot contradict itself, and because both gospels are recording Jesus's words, and Jesus cannot contradict himself, we must understand these two passages together. Matthew's "good things" must be understood in a way that is in keeping with Luke's "Holy Spirit" and vice versa. This means that the best understanding of what Jesus is saying in these two passages is something like "the Spirit and the good things of the Spirit" or, perhaps better, "Spiritual good things." In other words, Jesus is not merely saying that the Father will give us good things in answer to our prayers—although that is true—but defining the *kind* of good things that the Father will give us. He will give us *spiritual*—or, perhaps better, *Spiritual*—good things.

About twenty years ago, I attended a conference at which Joni Eareckson Tada was speaking. She talked about diving into the Chesapeake when she was seventeen years old and breaking her neck. She described what happened when she was lying in a hospital room afterward and how she poured out her heart to the Lord for healing. She talked about singing through tears the words of Fanny Crosby's hymn "Pass Me Not, O Gentle Savior" as a plea to the Lord to intervene:

> Pass me not, O gentle Savior,
> Hear my humble cry;

While on others Thou art calling,
Do not pass me by.[5]

Joni went on to say that for years she believed God had not answered her prayer because she was never healed. For years, she thought that God really had passed her by, consigning her to live in a wheelchair as a quadriplegic. But then she relayed how, decades after her time in the hospital, she went on a trip to Israel with her husband and, as a result, saw her prayer for healing in a completely different light. It was while she was visiting the pool of Bethesda—the place where the man who had been an invalid for thirty-eight years had been healed by the Lord (see John 5). Joni recounted how, as she sat in her wheelchair at the pool, the words of the prayer she had made in the hospital came flooding back to her. I'll never forget what she said next. She said that she realized then and there that a *no* answer to her prayer for physical healing had actually been a *yes* answer to her prayer. She realized that the Lord hadn't passed her by after all.[6]

The Lord answered Joni's prayers for healing, but he didn't answer them in the way she envisioned. In the language of Luke 11:13, he answered her prayers *Spiritually*. Whatever else God may have done in and through Joni's prayers, he certainly blessed her with incredible spiritual maturity and beauty and gave her a ministry and an influence that would never have been possible had he healed her physically all those years ago. The Lord answered Joni's prayer, but he didn't answer it in the way she expected or even wanted at the moment.

God is far more interested in spiritual healing and spiritual blessing than he is in physical healing and physical blessing. Sometimes, to be sure, he answers our prayers for physical healing and physical blessing by giving us exactly what we ask for. But we cannot expect him to do so every time we pray. Instead, we can expect that God will *always* give us Spiritual good things every time we pray, even if we don't specifically ask for them.

Earlier in this chapter I mentioned the man who had prayed for his wife to be healed for months on end only to have her taken from him. When he approached me after hearing me preach on prayer, he was discouraged and struggling with God's goodness. He wondered how anyone could say that God answers prayer. I told him then what I am writing now. I told him that God answers prayer—sometimes he does it by giving us what we ask for; sometimes he does it by giving us Spiritual good things instead. But he always answers. The man's pleading and his crying out to the Lord with tears were not in vain. His prayers didn't fall to the ground unanswered. God heard, and he answered from on high. He may not have answered in the exact ways that this man wanted, but he did answer. He may not have provided the fish that this man asked for, but he didn't give him a serpent, and he most assuredly gave him *Spiritual good things*. Maybe these good things included spiritual growth for the man and his children. Maybe they entailed the conversion of many lost souls to faith in Christ. Or maybe they involved some other spiritual good that has yet to come to pass. We may never know this side of heaven exactly how the Lord answered this man's prayers. But we do know that God answered his prayers, because Jesus promises us that God will always give Spiritual good things to his children when they cry out to him in prayer.

If Prayer Works, Then What?

The fact that God answers prayer means that we can pray with anticipation and expectation for what God will do in and through our prayers. No prayer is ever wasted. No prayer falls to the ground. God may not answer by giving us exactly what we have in mind, but he always answers by giving us Spiritual good things. We can pray with the expectation that our prayers really will do something good.

I realize that this teaching may be more challenging within some traditions than it is within others. Those who believe in the continuation of the extraordinary gifts of the Holy Spirit—gifts like speaking in tongues or healing—may pray with more expectation than those who come from a tradition similar to my own, which regards the continuation of these extraordinary gifts more suspiciously. Their convictions about the continuing work of the Holy Spirit groom them to look for God to answer their prayers, whereas Christians from backgrounds like mine often approach prayer with more hesitancy and doubt.[7] In my experience, people from within the Reformed tradition are often tempted to believe that today is a day of small things and not to expect God to do the kinds of mighty things that he did in the past.

For that reason, knowing that our God really does answer prayer, those of us who come from backgrounds like mine may need to be encouraged to pray for big things and for grand ideas and plans. God invites us to "open [our] mouth wide," as the psalmist says, and promises that he "will fill it" (Ps. 81:10). We are to hold nothing back from him. We are to ask *largely* and with great expectation that God will in fact answer largely.

C. H. Spurgeon was once serving as a guest preacher in a different congregation than his own. Before the beginning of his sermon, he prayed and asked the Lord to bring even one soul to faith in Christ through the message he was about to give. After the service, as he was eating at a church member's home, he was kindly rebuked for his lack of faith in asking for only one soul to be converted. The church member told him that with the greatness of the gospel message he was preaching and with the greatness of the crowd present, he ought to have asked for one thousand souls instead of just one. Thinking back on this rebuke, Spurgeon later concluded, "Many of us have made great mistakes and have shut ourselves up in the cells of poverty when our feet might have stood in a large room. We have laid down pipes too small to bring us a full current of blessing. Our cup is small, and we blame the fountain."[8]

Not only do we serve a great God who is all-powerful and altogether good, but we serve a God who has already given us the greatest gift he could possibly give—his Son Jesus. And having given us his Son, "how will he not also with him graciously give us all things?" (Rom. 8:32). Let us strive to ask largely, my friend. Let us open wide our mouths and ask for great things for the kingdom of God. Why? Because God answers prayer.

Questions for Further Reflection

1. Have you ever seemed to experience unanswered prayer? When? How did it make you feel?
2. How does this chapter help to address the matter of unanswered prayer? Do you find the discussion helpful or unhelpful? Why?
3. Why does the Bible not give us every qualification regarding prayer in one single passage?
4. What does it mean to pray "in Jesus's name"? "According to God's will"? With selfless motives? With genuine repentance?
5. Does God answer prayer? If so, what can you do practically to pray more yourself and to encourage those around you to do the same?

3

PRAYER IS NECESSARY

The Reformed and Presbyterian tradition has long placed a high value on the role of the Bible in the Christian life, and rightly so. We have strongly encouraged Christians to give themselves wholeheartedly to reading the Word and to sitting under the regular preaching of it. John Calvin famously referred to the Bible as a pair of glasses that alone can bring the world into proper focus.[1] His successors referred to it as the workshop of the Holy Spirit—that place in which God does his sanctifying work of rubbing off the rough edges in our lives.

It may be something of a surprise, therefore, that another Reformed author, J. C. Ryle, says that it is prayer, and not the reading or preaching of the Word, that is absolutely necessary for salvation: "It is not absolutely needful to salvation that a man should *read* the Bible. A man may have no learning, or be blind, and yet have Christ in his heart. It is not absolutely needful that a man should *hear* the public preaching of the Gospel. He may live where the Gospel is not preached, or he may be bedridden, or deaf. But the same thing cannot be said about prayer. It is absolutely needful to salvation that a man should *pray*."[2]

Why would Ryle put prayer in an altogether different category from Scripture and refer to prayer alone as being absolutely necessary to salvation? The answer that we give to this question will help us to see why it is so important that we prioritize prayer in our lives and ministries.

God Commands Prayer

Our first answer to the question *Why is prayer necessary?* is that God commands us to pray. First Thessalonians 5:17 exhorts us to "pray without ceasing," and Colossians 4:2 instructs us to "continue steadfastly in prayer, being watchful in it with thanksgiving." These passages, in addition to others like them, should be enough in and of themselves to convince us that we need to pray.

Prayer Is Spiritual Breathing

But as important as it is for us to remember that God commands us to pray—and, thus, that prayerlessness is disobedience—it must also be acknowledged that this doesn't get to the heart of the reason that prayer is "absolutely needful to salvation." We find that reason in the comparison Ryle makes between prayer and breathing: "Just as the first sign of life in an infant when born into the world, is the act of breathing, so the first act of men and women when they are born again, is *praying*."[3]

Breathing is indispensable for physical life. We can live only for short periods without it. No matter how adept we may be at holding our breath, we all must breathe at some point. And prayer, according to Ryle, operates the same way. We may "hold our breath" from time to time and experience seasons of prayerlessness, but sooner or later, if we are alive spiritually, we all must pray.

To look at it another way, praying is just as necessary for the Christian as growing oranges is for the orange tree. Every healthy orange tree will necessarily produce oranges. It may not produce as many oranges as it did in previous seasons or as many as other nearby trees produce. But it *will* produce oranges. If it doesn't, then there is something wrong with the tree. It is either dead, or it is not actually an orange tree after all. The lifeblood of the orange tree will necessarily overflow in the production of fruit in its branches.

In the same way, the new life that is within the Christian will necessarily overflow in prayer. Sometimes this "overflow" may produce more prayer than it has in past seasons of our lives, and sometimes it may produce less. Sometimes it may produce more for us than it does for others around us. The amount of prayer isn't as important as the presence of it.

We see this reality in Romans 8, for instance, when Paul first differentiates Christians from non-Christians by the presence of the Holy Spirit living within them, giving new life to their "mortal bodies" (see vv. 9–11), and then teaches that the same Holy Spirit "helps us" in our prayers by "interced[ing] for us with groanings too deep for words" (v. 26). The point is that the Spirit who inhabits every Christian overflows in the life of the believer in prayer. To use Ryle's language of breathing, this means that the Holy Spirit not only helps us to breathe but actually *ensures* that we will breathe, in the same way that the lifeblood of the orange tree ensures the production of oranges in the branches.

Acts 9 suggests something similar as well. In this passage, the Lord tells Ananias to go see Saul, one of the early church's most zealous persecutors, and to lay hands on him so that he may regain his eyesight after being struck blind on the road to Damascus. Because the Lord knows that Ananias will be concerned about putting his life at risk by doing this, he reassures him that Saul is no longer the same man. He has been changed on the road to Damascus. The man that Ananias is going to visit is now a Christian himself. The Lord gives Ananias the reassurance of this change in Saul in five words (only three in the original Greek): "For behold, [Saul] is praying" (Acts 9:11). The fact that Saul is praying is enough in and of itself to alleviate Ananias's fears and to convince him that Saul is no longer a persecutor of Christ but a follower instead. The new spiritual life in Saul manifests itself in prayer in the same way that the new life in an infant manifests itself in breathing or the new life in a tree manifests itself in fruit.

Prayer Is a Measure of Our Spiritual Condition

Barometers are instruments used to measure the atmospheric pressure in a given environment or location. I am told that they can be very useful in predicting the weather, insofar as rapid increases or decreases in the barometric pressure indicate that different weather systems are moving in and bringing either rain or sunshine with them. Barometers, therefore, help us to measure something that cannot be seen or discerned otherwise, and they show us what will happen in the immediate future if things continue as they are currently.

If prayer really is like breathing, then it functions in much the same way that a barometer does: it measures our spiritual condition, which cannot be seen or discerned otherwise, and it shows us what will happen in the immediate future if we continue without it. Persisting in prayerlessness is like persisting in holding our breath under water. If something doesn't change, we will soon die. Prayerlessness is thus a barometric pressure warning that something isn't right. It is a warning light flashing on the dashboard of our lives. We ignore it at our own peril.

A member of the church where I previously served used to enjoy playing a game with his car. He used to enjoy seeing how close he could get his gas tank to empty without ever actually running out of gas. Using the digital display on the dashboard to tell him how many miles he had remaining, he would ignore the yellow fuel light and would refuse to get gas until the last possible moment. I think he actually got the digital display down to "0 miles remaining" on one or two occasions. To my knowledge, he has never run out of gas and been left stranded on the side of the road, but, certainly, we would all acknowledge that it is only a matter of time before it happens.

This may be a fun game to play with a car, but it is not such a benign thing to try in the Christian life when the stakes are a lot higher. The point of the Christian life is not to ignore the yellow "warning light" and see how close to complete prayerlessness we can get. We run the risk of not simply being left stranded on the side of the road temporarily but of being left "stranded" in hell for eternity. Ongoing prayerlessness is at least a sign of a spiritual problem, and it may well be a sign of the complete absence of saving faith altogether.

Where Is the Encouragement in All This?

There are times in the Christian life when we may find it extremely hard to pray. We may even stay mired in these kinds of seasons for extended periods. Trials and tribulations, losses and crosses, can make it hard to do anything but put one foot in front of the other. In the congregation where I previously served, an older couple tragically lost both of their sons and their one daughter-in-law in a very short span of time. They wrestled with the Lord and struggled to understand why he would allow this kind of thing to happen. They found it extremely challenging to spend time with the Lord in prayer—and understandably so. Although you and I may not face the same exact circumstances as this couple, we all experience similar seasons when we find it hard to go to the Lord in prayer.

Seeing prayer as breathing can be tremendously encouraging in these kinds of seasons. We know from human experience that our bodies aren't always able to breathe with the same amount of strength and vitality. Sickness, disease, and trauma can significantly affect the quality of our breathing. In situations in which we struggle to breathe, we know that the *quality* of our breathing is not nearly as important as the *fact* that we are breathing. And the same is true in regard to prayer. The losses and crosses of the Christian life can affect our praying. Sometimes they can affect it so severely that the only thing we can do is cry out in our hearts with a one-word prayer: "Help!" Sometimes we may feel as though we are hyperventilating and can manage only short bursts of prayer as if we are gasping for breath. In moments like these, the quality of our prayers is not nearly as important as their presence. This ought to be tremendously encouraging for all of us.

Genuine faith manifests itself in prayer. It may not always manifest itself in the kind of prayer that spends an hour or more on our knees every day. But it will manifest itself. It may at times be small and barely noticeable. But it will be there. Seeing prayer as breathing can help to encourage us in this way, especially in those periods of life when all we can do is put one foot in front of the other.

Life Support Shouldn't Be a Permanent Option

But if our prayers stay "small and barely noticeable" and never grow beyond that stage, we have a different kind of problem. The same thing would be true of the individual who is always on life support. There may well be seasons for all of us in which we need help to breathe. But that isn't the ideal to shoot for. A person on a breathing machine clearly isn't the picture of health. A person who only ever prays one-word prayers isn't the picture of spiritual health either.

Comparing prayer to breathing, then, not only tells us why we should pray but also tells us that we should strive to grow in our ability to pray if we find ourselves on spiritual life support for extended seasons. The warning light on the dashboard is intended to get our attention. It is beckoning us to give the time and energy necessary to alleviate the problem by learning (or relearning) how to pray. (For more on this, see the questions and answers later on in the book.)

Prayer Is a Necessary Expression of Relationship

The Reformed and Presbyterian tradition has historically held that faith is relational. It consists of more than knowing relevant facts about Christ. It consists of the most intimate of relationships, even stronger than what exists between a husband and wife.[4]

John Calvin and Martin Luther both describe faith in terms of marriage love, even going so far as to apply the one-flesh language of Ephesians 5:22–33 to Christians in their relationship with Christ. Faith in Jesus means that we become "flesh of his flesh and bone of his bone."[5] For post-Reformation theologians like Samuel Rutherford, faith "layeth hold on relations, and such a relation as is betweene husband and wife."[6]

The idea that faith is a relationship means that, like all relationships, it requires ongoing care and attention. Prayer is a way that we give this care and attention to strengthen our relationship with God. As Samuel Rutherford once said, prayerlessness "deadens marriage-love."[7] It weakens the marriage bond that is ours with Christ through faith. Prayer is, therefore, a necessary manifestation of an ongoing faith relationship with God, and for that reason, prayer is "absolutely needful to salvation."

But the fact that faith is an intimate relationship also serves to highlight the incredible blessing that prayer provides. Intimacy in marriage between a man and woman is not only relational glue, as we saw previously, but also gloriously fun for each partner involved (or at least it should be!). It is not simply a means of procreation or a means of strengthening the relationship but also a tremendous blessing. To be sure, that blessing doesn't remove the work that intimacy entails, but it does make the work worthwhile, doesn't it? And the same can be said in regard to prayer. God has given us the incredible blessing of enjoying ongoing intimacy with him, the God of the universe. That blessing doesn't remove the work that prayer entails, but it does make the work worthwhile.

The One Who Has Been Loved Much Prays Much

The parable of the prodigal son in Luke 15:11–32 does not tell us what happened on the morning after the son returned home, was greeted by the lavish love of his father, and was regaled as the guest of honor at the feast celebrating his return. But I have to think that the son rose early in the morning to spend as much time as possible with his father. This is just what we would expect, isn't it? Having been loved much by his father, the son surely loved him much in return. The nature of love, after all—especially this kind of lavish, selfless love—is to attract and not to repel. When you and I experience this kind of love—which is precisely what we *have* experienced in and through Jesus Christ—we will necessarily be drawn to spend time with the One from whom this love so bountifully flows. If we aren't drawn to spend time with him, then something is wrong with our experience of his love.

This is precisely what Jesus is saying in Luke 7, when, while speaking to Simon the Pharisee about "a woman of the city, who was a sinner" (v. 37), he declares, "Therefore I tell you, her sins, which are many, are forgiven—for she loved much. But he who is forgiven little, loves little" (v. 47). This woman's experience of the love of God, which was significant insofar as she was forgiven much, overflowed and expressed itself in the way that she lived. But this wasn't the case in Simon's life, which clearly demonstrated that there was a problem in his experience of the love of God.

Consequently, the more we understand the depth and extent of the love of God that is ours in Christ, the more we will give ourselves to prayer. We have indeed been loved much, and, having been loved much, we will pray much in return, because the Father's love necessarily draws us to spend time with him. This means that meditating on the Father's love is a great way not only to encourage us in general but to encourage us specifically to pray.

Prayer Is Our Lifeline on the Battlefront

Paul teaches us in Ephesians 6:10–20 that our lives will be characterized by war—not war against earthly powers and armies but war against "the rulers, against the authorities, against the cosmic powers over this present darkness, [and] against the spiritual forces of evil in the heavenly places" (v. 12). The devil and all who do his bidding, Paul says, are seeking to thwart the Lord's work in the world by destroying his people, leading us astray, and rendering us ineffective.

But the Lord has not left us alone in our struggle. He has given everything we need to take our stand and fight. He has given us the "belt of truth," the "breastplate of righteousness," the "readiness" that comes from the "gospel of peace," the "shield of faith," the "helmet of salvation," and the "sword of the Spirit, which is the word of God" (vv. 14–17). What is more, he has also given us access to him in prayer. That is why Paul encourages us to give ourselves to "praying at all times in the Spirit, with all prayer and supplication" (v. 18). He knows that we are at war, and because we are, we need to be able to call in to our commanding General for help at every moment.

John Piper has helpfully referred to prayer as "a wartime walkie-talkie" that connects us to our commanding General and enables us to "call in firepower for conflict with a mortal enemy."[8] In speaking this way, Piper reminds us that we are not alone in our fight. It's not that God has given us everything we need to make our stand and then left us to fend for ourselves. God has given us everything we need, *and* he has also given us ongoing access to himself. We have access to his limitless supplies of wisdom, power, and grace. We have access to all that he is, in and of himself, whenever and wherever we may need it. And that is a tremendous blessing!

Prayer is necessary precisely because you and I are at war. God has given us prayer so that we can survive. It is our lifeline that connects us to him. When we realize that, we will be more motivated to give ourselves to prayer and, specifically, to kingdom-focused prayer. Praying for God's kingdom to come and his will to be done on earth as it is in heaven (see Matt. 6:10) is not simply an optional luxury when we are at war. It is an absolute necessity. It is life itself.

Given the importance of prayer as a lifeline to secure the help of our commanding General in our fight against Satan and his armies, it should be no surprise that the apostles give pride of place to the role of prayer in their exercise of leadership. They see that their primary responsibility is to "devote [themselves] to prayer and to the ministry of the word" (Acts 6:4). Note the order—first prayer, then the ministry of the Word. Since the apostles were also elders in the church (see 1 Peter 5:1), what they say about the place of prayer in their own ministries applies to all those who serve as elders. In fact, I would apply it to every follower of Jesus, because we are all called to some kind of ministry, whether that takes place within our group of friends, our family, our workplace or community, or our church.

If everything we have said about the nature of the Christian life and the role of prayer in it is true, then it makes sense that those who take up the mantle of leadership would give first place to prayer. The degree to which we don't is the degree to which we misunderstand what prayer is and why we should be doing it. Prayer is not *preparation for* the real work that leaders do. It *is* the real work. Prayer gives us access to God and to every help that we need to live the Christian life and to minister where God has placed us. For, as Paul said under the inspiration of the Holy Spirit, "we do not wrestle against flesh and blood, but against the rulers, against the authorities, against the cosmic powers over this present darkness, against the spiritual forces of evil in the heavenly places" (Eph. 6:12).

What Does This All Mean?

Because prayer is necessary, we should look for ways to encourage ourselves to engage in it. We can read books, like this one, that will motivate us to pray (that is certainly my goal anyway!). We can allow the events of our everyday lives to push us toward prayer. Seasons of hardship will remind us to roll our burdens upon the Lord (see Ps. 55:22), but good times and joys and successes ought to do this as well. *Every* providence in our lives ought to remind us to go to the Lord in prayer, either to ask for help and thank God for what he has done or to confess our failure when we neglect to do these things.

We can cultivate the practice of Godward living, so that everything in our lives is directed to the Lord. When we misplace our keys, we take it to the Lord in prayer. When we get cut off in traffic, we take it to the Lord in prayer. When our favorite college football team loses to its in-state rival—yes, I know that has gone from preaching to meddling!—we take it to the Lord in prayer. We use every opportunity to encourage ourselves to pray.

One of the things that I have sought to do in my own life to cultivate this Godward attitude is to pray immediately with everyone who shares something with me. When people tell me about a particularly challenging situation in their lives, I try to stop and pray with them right then and there, whether on the phone or in person. That keeps me from saying that I will pray for them and then forgetting to do so. But it also trains me to live Godwardly in all the details of my life.

The necessity of prayer also means that we look for accountability in our lives. And when I say *accountability,* I don't necessarily mean that we need to find people who will hold us accountable by constantly asking us if we are spending enough time in prayer—as helpful as that may be. What I principally have in mind when I speak of accountability is simply the practice of praying with other people. I have found that this practice provides a kind of built-in accountability for me to ensure that I am spending time every day in prayer. I like to meet with several different groups each week to pray. The staff at the seminary where I work meets every week to pray for one another and for the work we are doing. The house group that I lead at church meets every week to pray for one another and the things that are on our hearts. I pray with my family. I pray in my classes. I pray with the people I meet with throughout the day. You get the point. This is the kind of accountability that I find most helpful for encouraging me to pray.

The fact that prayer is a necessary fruit of saving faith indicates that we look for ways to grow in our fruitfulness. This means more than simply growing in the amount of time we spend in prayer. It means growing in the things we pray for and the way in which we pray for them. The more we grow in the Christian life, for instance, the more attention we ought to give to praying kingdom prayers, because growing in maturity means that we are being made more and more in conformity with God's will, and, as this happens, our prayers should also grow more and more in conformity with God's will.

We should do all these things, and more, to help to encourage us to pray because prayer really is "absolutely needful to salvation." Just as breathing is absolutely necessary to be physically alive, so praying is absolutely necessary to be spiritually alive. Once we understand that, we can readily see that asking ,"Why should we pray?" is a lot like asking, "Why should we breathe?"

Questions for Further Reflection

1. How is prayer like breathing? Do you find that to be a helpful analogy? Why or why not? How does it encourage you in seasons of prayerlessness?
2. Does the ability to breathe (i.e., pray) come from ourselves? Who or what is the source of our praying/breathing? How is this kind of breathing like the fruit that a healthy tree produces?
3. What does prayerlessness tell us about our spiritual condition?
4. Why is prayer a necessary overflow of being loved much by God?
5. How is prayer a "lifeline"? How does this idea apply practically to life and ministry?

4

GROWING IN PRAYER

If you have ever planted seeds in order to watch them grow, you will have noticed that certain things happen as those seeds sprout and develop. The single stem that initially shoots up through the surface of the soil soon acquires leaves and eventually blossoms into a full-grown plant or tree. The same is true in regard to prayer. As we grow, certain things happen in our lives.

We Know Better How to Break Up the Icy Layer of Our Hearts

One of the first things to happen as we grow in prayer is that we come to understand more of what it takes to stir our hearts to pray. Very few of us wake up each day ready to plead with the Lord in prayer. More typically, we wake up feeling as though that thin layer of ice has formed around our hearts. This icy layer freezes our affections and renders us incapable of doing the heart work that prayer requires. I have found that I need to break up this icy layer by meditating on a passage of Scripture, listening to a rousing sermon, or reading something that will remind me of what Christ has done for me, of who I am in Christ, or of the tremendous privilege and power of prayer. Christian biographies and books on prayer have been particularly helpful for me in this regard. Reading about the prayer lives of Christians from previous generations—men like George Müller, John G. Paton, David Brainerd, Hudson Taylor, and Charles Simeon, for instance, who were giants in prayer—and being reminded through their lives that God really does answer prayer has encouraged me to devote more time and energy to this endeavor, especially in those moments when I may not feel like doing so.

These are some of the things that have worked for me. But I realize that it may take something different for others of my brothers and sisters. No two of us are exactly the same, which means that each of us has to learn what works best for ourselves. We do this as we grow in prayer. We begin to learn how best to administer the jolt of caffeine that our hearts so often require before they can be poured out in prayer. And once we learn this, we need to put these lessons into practice.

We Are Careful about Who We Pray with and How Often

Because prayer involves pouring out our hearts before the Lord, we should also be careful about who we pray with and how often we do it. For example, as a pastor I have had a number of newly engaged couples come see me in my office and confess that they have been sleeping together. In each situation, I've discovered that these couples were spending significant time together each day in prayer. They did this because they thought it was the right thing to do to give a spiritual dimension to their relationship. In each of these situations, I told them that they should not have been praying together—at least not in a sustained way—until they were married. I told them this because prayer is itself intimate communion. When we engage in it rightly, we pull back the veil from our hearts and stand before the throne of God vulnerable and spiritually naked. When we do this with another person of the opposite sex on a regular basis, our hearts can become knit together with that person through the shared experience of spiritual intimacy. Why are we so surprised when, after sharing this kind of regular spiritual intimacy, two people are less able to resist sharing physical intimacy as well, especially when they are so close to being married?

I am not suggesting that two people of the opposite sex can never pray together unless they are married. They absolutely can and should pray together. But I am suggesting that they should probably not pray together alone by themselves for a significant period of time on a regular basis without putting some kinds of limitations or protections in place. That is typically a recipe for disaster. Prayer is a bonding experience that necessarily knits together the hearts of those who engage in it. This, too, is something we learn as we grow in prayer.

We Strengthen the Church, and the Church Strengthens Us

It is precisely because prayer is a bonding experience, however, that churches and ministries ought to devote themselves to it. The familiar adage really is true: "The church that prays together stays together." Could it be that one of the reasons why so many people today are hopping from church to church is because churches are not praying together as a whole, and, as a result, they lack the bonding that the intimacy of prayer alone can provide? There is no doubt that Jesus taught his disciples to pray "*our* Father" instead of "*my* Father" and to ask the Lord to "give *us*," "forgive *us*," "lead *us*," and "deliver *us*" (Matt. 6:9, 11–13). By doing so, he indicated that the intimacy of prayer was to be a shared experience—not only in terms of knitting our hearts together but also in terms of building a communal attitude and approach to life. We need one another to live the Christian life, and corporate prayer expresses and solidifies this reality.

Praying with other believers can also help us to engage in prayer when we don't feel like it. Not only does it provide built-in accountability, but it also helps us to break the icy layer around our hearts by exposing us to the heat produced from the hearts of others with whom we are praying. In this sense, corporate prayer is a lot like standing in the sunshine when we are shivering. The sun warms us up and takes away all our coldness.

When my wife and I were living in Scotland, we visited a church in Glasgow one Sunday for the regular morning worship service. When we arrived, the service had already started, and the minister could be heard praying over the speakers in the foyer as we entered the building. Even as we stood waiting in the foyer, I felt my own heart being lifted up to heaven by the minister's prayer. The heartfelt and heart-filled pleading, the scriptural content, and the humility and familiarity of his prayer warmed my heart and prepared me to pray and worship. That is what corporate prayer does. It knits our hearts together within the church and lifts us up to heaven together, and both the church and its members are the stronger for it.

We Experience Encouragement Together as God's People

One of my favorite moments in C. S. Lewis's *The Lion, the Witch and the Wardrobe* is the occasion in which Mr. Beaver first mentions Aslan's name to Peter, Susan, Edmund, and Lucy in Narnia. Leaning in close to the four children, he whispers, "They say Aslan is on the move." Their reaction is immediate: "The moment the Beaver had spoken these words everyone felt quite different. . . . At the name of Aslan each one of the children felt something jump in his inside."[1] This same expression—"Aslan is on the move"—is repeated at other times in the story to encourage and embolden the citizens of Narnia to remain faithful in the midst of difficulty. It reminds them that Aslan is not only aware of their troubles but actively engaged in doing something about them even if they do not fully see it at the moment.

The simple fact that prayer works does the same for us. It tells us that God is on the move as we pray. He not only is aware of our troubles but also is actively engaged in doing something about them in answer to our prayers. We may not know exactly what God is doing, but we do know that he is acting in keeping with his character and purposes. We know this because prayer works. It may not always work in the way that we expect or intend. But when we pray, God is on the move, and that is just as much a source of encouragement for us as it was for the characters in Lewis's Narnia.

Because God moves as we pray, you and I have the tremendous privilege of being colaborers with the God of the universe (see 1 Cor. 3:9). God is using even our imperfect, sometimes shallow, mostly feeble prayers to accomplish his perfect purposes in the world. This, too, is an encouragement. But it brings with it an important responsibility—the responsibility to "keep in step with the [Holy] Spirit" (Gal. 5:25). If the same Holy Spirit who lives within us also helps us to pray, especially when we don't know what to pray for, and intercedes—or, we might even say, prays—for us "with groanings too deep for words" (Rom. 8:26; see also Zech. 12:10), then when we pray, we are keeping in step with the Spirit, because the Spirit is himself a Spirit of prayer. And, correspondingly, when we refuse to pray, we are quenching the Holy Spirit (see 1 Thess. 5:19).

This means that you and I will cultivate a sensitivity to the Spirit's promptings within us as we grow more and more in prayer. When the Spirit lays it upon our hearts to pray, we will see it as evidence that God wants to move in some way in the world around us and wants us to be a part of it by way of our prayers. We will ask the Lord to bring to our minds the things or the people whom he wants us to pray for as we lie awake at night, unable to sleep. This, too, happens as we grow in prayer.

We Pray Kingdom Prayers with a Greater Sense of Urgency

Furthermore, as we grow in prayer, we begin to realize that we are living in spiritual warfare, and, therefore, we start praying for different things. We find ourselves praying less for those things that will only make our earthly lives easier and more comfortable and praying more for spiritual things pertaining to the kingdom of the Lord Jesus Christ. We pray for the necessary strength and resources to keep on fighting the good fight, for God's kingdom not only to hold its ground but also to advance and reclaim territory, and for Satan and his army to be defeated once and for all. In other words, we pray for God's kingdom to come and for his will to be done on earth as it is in heaven (see Matt. 6:10).

And as we grow in prayer, we pray for these things with a renewed sense of urgency, longing to see the victory fulfilled at last. We cry out with the apostle John, "Come, Lord Jesus!" (Rev. 22:20; see also 2 Tim. 4:8). Come and make all things right. Come and bring an end to everything that stands in opposition to you. Come and usher in the new heavens and the new earth and, in doing so, "wipe away every tear" from our eyes and vanquish the "former things" once and for all (Rev. 21:4). Like the man in Luke 11, we ask and keep on asking until we receive, we seek and keep on seeking until we find, and we knock and keep on knocking until the door is at last opened to us.

We Turn the World Upside Down

In his book *Christ's Call to Discipleship,* James Montgomery Boice lays down an effective challenge, calling Christians to take up our crosses and to follow after Christ with all that we are and have. To summarize what could happen if an entire generation of Christians embraced this challenge and began following after Christ in the way that he describes in his book, Boice says, "That generation by the power of God could transform the world."[2]

Even though Boice is speaking specifically about discipleship, his words could easily apply to what I have been saying about prayer. As we grow in prayer, we understand more of what it is, what it does, and why it is necessary, and we begin to give ourselves to it more and more. We open our mouths wide, we pray large prayers (see Ps. 81:10), and we do so with persistence and pleading. If the church could produce a generation of men and women who are characterized by these things, that generation by the power of God could undoubtedly transform the world. As we grow in prayer, we begin to reclaim the priority of prayer in our lives and ministries, and as a result, we grow into the kind of people the Lord can use to turn the world upside down (see Acts 17:6). I invite you to join me in praying—and in praying specifically to that end.

Questions for Further Reflection

1. What are some of the practical ways you have found to overcome the resistance to prayer that we all sometimes feel?
2. What protections ought we to consider putting in place when praying with someone of the opposite sex? Why might this be important?
3. How should prayer express and solidify the corporate aspects of our salvation? What does that mean practically for your own prayer life?

4. How does corporate prayer encourage us to pray more frequently, more fervently, and for bigger things?
5. What does the Bible lead us to expect if Christians give themselves wholeheartedly to prayer? What are some of the ways you can apply this in your own life and church?

QUESTIONS AND ANSWERS ON PRAYER

Before any of us can ever give ourselves to the practice of persistent prayer, we must first understand why it is important to do so. Throughout this book I've tried to make a case for prayer that will help us to do just that. However, several questions may still remain. In what follows, therefore, I've tried to provide short(ish!) answers to some of the most common questions that may yet be lingering in your mind. There are recommended resources at the end of this book that can take you further still if you find that this section hasn't quite addressed all your questions.

If God is sovereign, why should I pray?

While this is a difficult question, the more difficult question for me is "If God is *not* sovereign, why should I pray?" Prayer is a colossal waste of time if God is not able to do anything about our situation. If God cannot change our circumstances or intervene in a definitive way, then praying to him for help can serve only a therapeutic purpose. It can comfort us by providing a listening ear, but it cannot ultimately effect any real change.

There are at least four reasons that we should pray to our sovereign God.

First, we are to pray because God commands us to do so. We are told, for example, to "pray without ceasing" in 1 Thessalonians 5:17 and to "be constant in prayer" in Romans 12:12. The Bible teaches us that prayer is a matter of obedience to God.

Second, we pray because we are following the example that Jesus set for us when he was on the earth. If Jesus gave himself to prayer, and if Christlikeness is the standard of our sanctification (see 1 Cor. 11:1; Phil. 3:10, 17; Col. 1:27), then we should give ourselves to the same endeavor. The sovereignty of God did not deter Jesus from praying—why should it deter us?

Third, we pray because prayer is the language of faith. It is the way that faith expresses itself. Just as physical life and breathing go together, so spiritual life and praying go together. A Christian who doesn't pray is a contradiction in terms.

Fourth, we pray because God is a God of means. God is able to do whatever he wants to do, whenever and however he wants to do it. He can bring his purposes to pass wholly on his own without using secondary causes or agents, like you or me or our prayers. But he typically does that only in extraordinary circumstances. More ordinarily, God works in and through the prayers and the actions of his people. So we pray because God is changing us, changing things, and changing the course of events in the world through our prayers.

It is fascinating to see how many of the major events of the Bible occur in response to prayer. Take the plagues in Egypt as an example. Most of them come or are lifted in response to the prayers of Moses. The Lord uses the prayers of Joshua to make the sun stand still at Gibeon (see Josh. 10:12–13). He uses the prayers of Elijah to bring drought and then, three and a half years later, to bring rain (see James 5:17–18). Over and over again in the Bible God uses prayer as the means of bringing his perfect purposes to pass. He doesn't have to do that. He is all-powerful, all-wise, and all-knowing. He is sovereign over all. But he is also a God who uses the prayers and the actions of his people to bring his sovereign purposes to pass.

Should prayer always be addressed to the Father?

Prayer does not always have to be addressed to the Father. It is perfectly appropriate to address our prayers to the Son and to the Holy Spirit too. All three persons of the Trinity are God. They are, to borrow the words of the Westminster Shorter Catechism, "the same in substance, equal in power and glory."[1] That means all three persons of the Trinity are rightly the recipients of our prayers and our praises. We can direct our prayers to the Father or to the Son or to the Holy Spirit.

Since each person of the Godhead is ascribed a unique mission in the Bible, it is appropriate to direct the prayers that are most in accord with a particular person's mission to that particular member of the Trinity. For instance, if we are praying for someone to come to faith in Christ, it would be appropriate to address that particular prayer to the Holy Spirit, because the Spirit's unique mission in Scripture is to apply the finished work of Christ to the hearts and minds of individuals.

That being said, however, the overarching pattern by which we approach God in salvation can also rightly be applied to our prayers. In salvation, we come *to* the Father, *through* the Son, *by the power* of the Holy Spirit. Since this is the way that we approach God in salvation, it is probably best for our prayers to follow this same pattern in general. We pray to the Father, through (or in the name of) Christ, by the power of the Holy Spirit.

Do I have to kneel down to pray?

No particular posture or stance is required for prayer. You can pray lying down, standing up, kneeling, sitting, walking, driving, and so on. In fact, if we really are going to "pray without ceasing" (1 Thess. 5:17), we will pray in every posture and position in which we find ourselves during the day.

That said, certain positions may be more conducive to prayer than others. For instance, you may find you fall asleep in the middle of your prayers when you try to pray lying down, or your mind may drift more easily when you are walking or driving. I have personally found that kneeling helps me to focus my mind and heart on the business of prayer. My mind wanders less, my heart is more engaged, and my prayers are more filled with reverence and praise when I kneel than when I take any other position. You may find that a different posture works better for you. That is great. Find what works for you and do it.

How can I learn to pray?

One of my seminary professors used to say that preaching is "better caught than taught." He meant that preaching is best learned by experience outside the classroom. The same can be said about prayer. Books and classroom lectures can help us. But we learn best to pray by listening to others pray and by doing it ourselves.

With this in mind, I would recommend five things to help Christians to learn to pray.

- *Listen to other people pray.* Listen especially to mature, seasoned Christians who have been through their share of hardship. Give heed to the words they use and the way they pray. Pay attention to your pastor when he prays in worship or in your hearing.
- *Read the Psalms.* Many of the Psalms are themselves prayers; most of the rest include prayers at some point. This is another way of "listening" to

mature Christians, to the words that they use and the ways in which they use them.

- *Memorize Scripture.* If praying "according to the will of God" means that we pray according to the *revealed* will of God, then there is no better way to do this than by memorizing that revealed will and adopting its language as our own.
- *Meditate on your sin and the work of Christ on your behalf.* John Bunyan has a fascinating section in his treatise on prayer in which he argues that men, women, and children learn best how to pray not by memorizing forms of prayer but by being convicted of their sins. He says that learning forms of prayer will only lead us to become prideful hypocrites who pray with our lips and our words rather than with our hearts. But being convicted of our sins "will make tears run down" from our eyes and "hearty groans flow" from our hearts.[2] In other words, it will cause us to pour out our hearts to the Lord, which, as we have seen, is really the essence of all prayer.
- *Pray.* Any method of learning to pray is of limited value if we don't actually pray ourselves. Set aside time to pray by yourself each day. Pray with your spouse and your kids. Start a prayer group at church or at school. Ask a friend to be a prayer partner. Give time and attention to praying, because prayer really is better caught than taught.

How can I overcome my fear of praying in public?

Most of us, at least at some point in our lives, have struggled with the fear of praying in public. Not long ago, I was asked to pray during one of the evening worship services for my denomination's General Assembly. Even after years of praying in public, I was nervous as I faced the crowd of four thousand or so people.

Fear is not necessarily a bad thing in and of itself. If our fear causes us to depend more heavily on the Lord than on our own strength, ability, or eloquence, then it is better to fear than not. If it causes us to pray more and to trust God more, then it is far better to be afraid than to be naturally confident or bold. But if our fear keeps us from praying or speaking or acting, or if it is motivated by an inordinate desire to please others, then it is not a good thing.

This means that the first step of overcoming our fear of praying in public is to pray in private. We plead with God to deliver us from our fear or to give us the strength to step out in faith despite the fear. And then we trust God, step out in faith, and pray in public. God may remove all our fears in the exact moment that we stand up to pray. Or he may not, and we may stumble and bumble our way through it. Either way, we will grow through the process. We will grow in our ability to trust the Lord and walk by faith in the midst of fear; and we will become less afraid the more we face our fears and step out in faith.

Nothing will help us to conquer our fear of praying in public the way that facing those fears will. Pray in private, trust God, and stand up and pray in public. Be strong and courageous in doing this. The Lord will honor your courage and will meet you at the point of your need. He certainly has in my own life.

What does it mean to pray in the Spirit?

Praying in the Spirit refers to praying in the power of the Spirit. Its opposite is praying in the flesh. When we pray in the flesh, we use our own strength to push our prayers forward. We rely on our own efforts, our own eloquence, and our own emotion to compensate for the deadness or coldness we may otherwise feel. But praying in the Spirit relies on the strength of the Holy Spirit for the words to say *and* for the power with which to say them.

The difference is similar to the difference between pushing and being pulled. When we push something, we use our own strength to do the work and move that object forward. But when we are being pulled by someone else, we can rest in the strength of the other person. The other person is doing the work. Similarly, the Holy Spirit helps us to pray by "pulling" us forward, giving us the words to say and the fervency with which to say them. He is, after all, explicitly called "the Helper" on a number of occasions in the Bible (see John 14:16, 26; 15:26; 16:7). One of the ways he fulfills this role is by helping us to pray, as Paul makes plain in Romans 8:26: "We do not know what to pray for as we ought, but the Spirit himself intercedes for us with groanings too deep for words."

What does praying in the Spirit look like?

Since the role of the Holy Spirit includes convicting us of our sin (see John 16:8), praying in the Spirit consists, first, of acknowledging our sin and our failures. This includes not only confessing our sins but also admitting our failures and inabilities in regard to prayer. We go before the Lord in a posture of humility on account of our sins and gratitude for the redemption that is ours in Christ, and we appeal to the Holy Spirit to overcome our self-reliance and general ineptitude in prayer. This awareness of our sins and failures ensures that we go before the Lord with inward groans and tears, which are indispensable parts of every prayer that seeks to pour out our hearts to the Lord.

Since the role of the Holy Spirit also includes leading us into truth (see John 14:17, 26; 15:26), praying in the Spirit also entails filling our prayers with Scripture and highlighting the person and work of Christ. The Bible says that Jesus is "the truth" (John 14:6), and this means that Spirit-empowered prayer necessarily points to who Jesus is and what he has done. And because the Bible, from beginning to end, points to the person and work of Christ (i.e., it is truth about the Truth), that means our prayers must also be filled with Scripture. When we pray in the Spirit, we rely on him to bring to our minds certain portions of God's Word as we pray—the obvious implication being that we need to know God's Word before the Spirit is able to call it to mind (insert plug for Scripture memorization!). Spirit-empowered prayer prays the promises of God and uses the language of God to do so.

Since the role of the Holy Spirit also entails intimacy with the Father—it is by the Spirit that we cry, "Abba! Father!" (Rom. 8:15)—Spirit-empowered prayer also involves intimate communion with God. It is an expression of the intimacy that is ours by way of the Spirit and strengthens that intimacy as well. There ought, therefore, to be a degree of familiarity, honesty, and heart engagement in our prayers as opposed to the distance and disconnectedness we so often evidence when we pray. This is why genuine prayer sometimes won't use any words at all. We pour out our hearts to the Lord, and words are certainly not always required to do this.

Is it *necessary* for Christians to pray in tongues?

While some traditions may advocate or even expect that Christians pray in tongues, the Bible doesn't seem to take this position. There is no explicit passage anywhere in the Bible that states that every Christian ought to engage in praying in tongues. Paul's comments in 1 Corinthians 14:18–19 suggest that the apostle himself used tongues in private prayer. But this should not be taken to indicate that every Christian today ought to follow the same practice. I say this for two main reasons.

First, Paul's emphasis in 1 Corinthians 14 is on tongue speaking not in private but in public. Thus he speaks about the "prophets" who are speaking in tongues when they "come together . . . in church" (see vv. 26–30). That suggests that the idea of praying in tongues in private cannot be wholly separated from the phenomenon of speaking in tongues in the public assembly. In this way, Paul emphasizes edification both in public and in private, and, thus, he requires the tongues spoken in both contexts to be interpreted (see vv. 13–19). This discourages the practice of praying in tongues unless the same individual can and does provide an interpretation at the same time. Otherwise, as Paul says, we would be praying with our spirits alone when we should be praying with both our spirits and our minds (see vv. 14–15).

Second, there is no one gift in the Bible that is intended for all Christians. Gifts are distributed variously in the church. That is part and parcel of what it means to be the body of Christ, which is Paul's whole point in 1 Corinthians 12. Some are eyes; some are ears; some are fingers; and some are toes. Later in the chapter, Paul applies this idea when he asks the rhetorical question "Do all speak with tongues?"—plainly assuming a reply in the negative (v. 30).[3] This means that it cannot be necessary for every Christian to pray in tongues.

When Paul says, "I want you all to speak in tongues" (1 Cor. 14:5) and "I thank God that I speak in tongues more than all of you" (1 Cor. 14:18), the "all" in both cases must be understood in light of the truth presented above in 1 Corinthians 12:30. As Richard Gaffin so helpfully observes, the "all" in 1 Corinthians 14 must be taken hypothetically, in the same way that it is in 1 Corinthians 7:7, where Paul says, "I wish that all were as I myself am. But each has his own gift from God, one of one kind and one of another." The diversity of gifts in the church must inform how we understand the "all" in 1 Corinthians 14, which tells us that Paul is not saying that all people should be speaking or praying in tongues.[4]

Is fasting required when we pray?

In the Bible, fasting is a sacrificial, voluntary abstaining from food (and sometimes from drink) for a definite period of time for a spiritual purpose. It rarely, if ever, occurs in the Bible as a stand-alone endeavor. In other words, it is not a practice that God's people engage in by itself but something that they do in conjunction with prayer.

Some fasts in Scripture are total abstentions, where both food and water are avoided (see Est. 4:16). Others are partial abstentions, where certain aspects of a normal diet are avoided for a given period (see Dan. 1:12; 10:3). Sometimes fasts in the Bible last for a whole day (see Lev. 16:29; 23:32) or for many days in a row (see Deut. 9:9–29; 10:1–11; Est. 4:16; Matt. 4:2). But sometimes they only last for a portion of a day (see Judg. 20:26; Dan. 6:18). The point is not that we abstain from a certain thing for a certain amount of time but instead that we deny ourselves in some way and devote ourselves to prayer. It is about using the time, energy, and focus that we would have used for eating (and/or drinking) to prayerfully seek the Lord.

The Bible doesn't require us to fast every time we pray, but it does assume that we will fast and pray on occasion. In Matthew 6:16, for instance, Jesus teaches his disciples by saying *when* (or *as often as*) you fast, not *if* you fast. In other words, by phrasing his instructions in the way that he does, Jesus assumes his followers will be fasting, just as he also assumes they will be giving to the poor (see v. 2) and praying (see vv. 5–7).

Why should we consider fasting when we pray?

Jesus's own example of fasting and his assumptions about the lives of his followers ought to be reason enough for us to adopt the practice of fasting ourselves. But God, in his great mercy, has provided many additional reasons for believers to embrace this practice. I will give six of them.

- *To show our earnestness.* Fasting helps us to express earnestness in our prayers (see 2 Chron. 20:3; Est. 4:16; Acts 14:23). By denying ourselves food, we are telling the Lord that we mean business—that we are putting our money where our mouth is, so to speak. We are showing him that we are ready to sacrifice anything—even ourselves—for the sake of our prayers.

- *To express our wholehearted faith in seeking the Lord.* In the Bible, fasting is often an expression of wholehearted devotion to God. It is a way of showing that we really are repentant and that he really is more important to us than mere physical pleasures (see Joel 2:12–13).
- *To plead with the Lord.* At other times in Scripture, fasting is an expression of mourning—either over death (see 2 Sam. 12:16) or over sin (see Jonah 3:5)—and of pleading with the Lord to hear our prayers for mercy and for healing (see Est. 9:31; Joel 1:14; Jonah 3:5).
- *To seek wisdom and guidance.* It is appropriate to pray and fast in the midst of daunting tasks and overwhelming situations in which we need wisdom and guidance. In 2 Chronicles 20:1–30, Jehoshaphat proclaims a national fast for this purpose as an enemy military horde advances.
- *To express humble reliance on the Lord.* In Ezra 8:21–23, a fast is proclaimed as an expression of humility and dependence on God for his provision. Fasting demonstrates that the people believe God will hear their prayers and provide what they need when they need it.
- *To prepare ourselves against temptation.* In Matthew 4:1–3, Jesus fasts so that he might be able to *withstand* the devil's temptations—not so that he might be weakened and the devil might be better

able to tempt him, as some may think. If Jesus fasted to be better prepared for temptation, how much more should we?

Is fasting a way to manipulate God and get what we want?

Fasting cannot manipulate God into answering our prayers or showing us mercy. It is not a hunger strike to ensure that God will meet our list of demands. It is a way of expressing our love for him and our gratitude for all that he has done for us. It is a way of communing with him and keeping our hearts fixed on him. The world continually seeks to pull our desires away from the Lord. It continually beckons us to find our pleasure in food or drink or other worldly delights. Fasting reminds us that the Lord is our chief pleasure, and it trains us to keep it that way. It helps us to remember that "fullness of joy" and "pleasures forevermore" can be found only in his presence and at his right hand (Ps. 16:11). Fasting plays an important role in the battle for our desires, and we neglect it to our own detriment.[5]

How long should I pray?

The Bible nowhere states how long Christians should pray. No doubt this is because God is more interested in our hearts than he is in mere outward obedience. If the Bible told us how long we should pray, you and I would pray for that amount of time and no more. Our hearts would probably not be engaged either. We would be watching the clock so that we could check the box and be satisfied that we had done our duty.

My wife doesn't give me a checklist of things that she wants me to do to show her that I love her. She wants my heart, and she wants me to act accordingly. She doesn't want me to do the minimum that I have to do. She desires that I lavish my love on her—and the same is true for God. He seeks our hearts, and he expects that we will pray accordingly.

When we look at the examples of prayer given in the Bible, we find both short and long prayers. In teaching his disciples to pray, Jesus gives them words to use that would take even the slowest among us less than a minute to utter (see Matt. 6:9–13). The Psalms frequently contain prayers that are no longer than a verse or two. And the father of the boy with the unclean spirit cries out with a prayer that consists of only five words: "I believe; help my unbelief" (Mark 9:24). But we also see Jesus praying for three hours in the garden of Gethsemane (see Matt. 26:40, 44), for approximately ten hours before he walks on the water (see Matt. 14:23, 25), and for the entire night before he calls his disciples to follow him (see Luke 6:12).

Prayer is an expression of intimacy with God that is similar to the intimacy that we experience in marriage. This tells us that we ought to take time for sustained prayer in our Christian lives. We wouldn't think of speaking only five words to our spouses on a regular basis. The relationship requires a deeper and more sustained level of intimacy. If we always pray short prayers and never have sustained periods of intimacy with the Lord, our relationship with him will be affected. Over time, it will lack the depth and resiliency that we may have seen in many older saints and longed to experience for ourselves.

How much of each day should be devoted to prayer?

The Bible calls us to "pray without ceasing" (1 Thess. 5:17). This doesn't mean that we have to spend every minute of every day in prayer. God has given all of us responsibilities and relationships that we have to attend to. Neglecting them in order to be alone in prayer with the Lord for every waking minute of every day would be wrong. My wife has enjoyed reminding me of this over the years by using a phrase she borrowed from some good friends of ours: "That is all well and good, but the trash still needs to go out." When she says this, she is reminding me that I cannot (and should not) spend all day in prayer and Bible study and think that I am being faithful. God has given me other responsibilities. Faithfulness involves stewarding *everything* that the Lord has given to me and *everything* that he expects of me.

Praying "without ceasing" means that we live every day prayerfully or, we might say, in a Godward direction. In other words, we are to use every detail of our lives, every relationship, every activity, and every responsibility to direct our attention and our prayers to the Lord. We are to pray about everything, during everything, and after everything. We are to live Godwardly in every detail of our lives. Sometimes this entails praying one-word prayers as we cry out to the Lord for help in difficult circumstances. Sometimes it involves praying with and for people who we meet throughout the course of the day. Sometimes it includes expressing our gratitude to the Lord for providential encouragements and blessings. The whole point is to use everything in our lives to direct our hearts and minds to God in prayer.

Is it wrong to pray for the same things over and over again?

It can be, but doesn't have to be, wrong to pray for the same things over and over again in our lives. In Matthew 6:7–8, Jesus condemns the "Gentiles," who "heap up empty phrases" when they pray, because "they think that they will be heard for their many words." The fact that the Gentiles use many words—and possibly repeat themselves over and over again—isn't the problem. Jesus isn't condemning them for their many words. He is condemning them for their motives: they think that God will hear them *because* of their many words. This means that if we are praying for the same things over and over again and are doing so with wrong motives—thinking that God will hear us the longer we pray and the more words we use—then it would be wrong to continue asking for them.

In other situations, it is clearly inappropriate to keep asking for the same things over and over again in prayer. In 2 Corinthians 12, for example, we are told that Paul prays three times for the "thorn in the flesh" to be taken away from him. He doesn't pray any more than this, because God has answered his prayer by saying, "My grace is sufficient for you" (v. 9). In this situation, it would be inappropriate for Paul to keep asking for the same thing after God has revealed his intentions to him, because he would be praying for something that is contrary to the revealed will of God. That is never appropriate for us to do.

With these caveats in mind, I would say in general that it is not wrong to ask God for the same things repeatedly. That is part and parcel of what it means to pray with persistence. Isaac apparently prayed for the same thing for twenty years—namely, for his wife Rebekah to get pregnant (see Gen. 25:20–21, 26). The man in Luke 11 didn't ask his neighbor for bread once and then go home. He asked and kept on asking for the same thing until he got it. And Jesus instructed his disciples that they "ought always to pray and not lose heart," even if it means "cry[ing out] to him day and night" for the same things (Luke 18:1, 7).

Is there anything that I shouldn't pray for?

It is never appropriate to pray for things that are contrary to God's revealed will. This means that we ought never to pray for injustice or for God's help in committing sin. God has commanded us to love justice and to pursue it and to forsake all sin. These things are all explicitly revealed to us in the Bible.

Is it wrong to use written prayers in private worship?

Using written prayers can be a valuable practice in private worship. They can help us to grow in our knowledge of and our facility with the language of prayer. They can provide helpful structure to our seasons of sustained prayer and keep our minds from wandering. But they ought never to completely replace our own personally generated prayers. Written prayers can keep us from pouring out our hearts before the Lord. They can devolve into a mindless exercise in which we recite words without ever thinking about what we are saying. If used long enough in this way, they can prevent us from praying on our own.

As we have seen previously, Christianity is a heart religion. God wants all of our heart, soul, mind, and strength (see Matt. 22:37–38). Prayer should thus be an overflow of our hearts—an expression of the intimate relationship between ourselves and the God of the universe. Written prayers make this kind of praying difficult, especially if we are relying on them exclusively in our Christian lives.

Is it wrong to use written prayers in corporate, public worship?

Written prayers may be more helpful in corporate worship than they are in private worship. They not only teach us the language of prayer, as we have seen, but also allow us to participate in prayer together, owning praise, thanksgiving, confession, and supplication for ourselves. The same dangers persist with the use of written prayers in corporate worship as in private, but corporate reciting of prayer may keep our hearts and minds more engaged than when we are simply listening to a minister or elder pray from the front.

However, I do not advise worship leaders to use written prayers when they pray in front of the congregation. I say this for several reasons.

First, it is very difficult to pour out our hearts before the Lord when we use written prayers. Part of leading in prayer is modeling what prayer should be like—both in terms of the words we use and the way we use them. Like it or not, congregations begin to pray the way their leaders do. Over time, they adopt the same phraseology, the same mannerisms, and the same energy (or lack thereof) that they see and hear in their leaders. This means that worship leaders are most effective when modeling prayer that involves all of the heart, mind, soul, and strength—and this is hard to do if we are reading prayers that we have written out.

Second, written prayers usually sound written. They use language that we would not ordinarily use in normal conversation. This can work to stifle prayer within a congregation rather than to cultivate it. Church members may be intimidated by the flowery words and the eloquent turns of phrase and lose heart because they cannot pray as flawlessly. Moreover, written prayers are usually read aloud before the congregation, which makes it difficult to communicate intimacy with the Lord in any way, shape, or form.

Third, written prayers provide a greater temptation for leaders to craft their prayers with an eye to impressing their hearers. This temptation accompanies any public prayer (see Matt. 6:5–6). But it is especially acute with written prayers, not simply because they involve premeditation but because, by the very nature of the medium, they also encourage us to concentrate on the words that we are using and how those words flow together.

For all these reasons, I am convinced that it is best for leaders to avoid using written prayers when praying in public worship or in any public forum. Instead, I favor what I would call *studied extemporaneous* prayer. Rather than standing up and saying whatever comes into their minds without any preparation or forethought, leaders ought to study and think through what they want to say beforehand (but not memorize), ensure that their hearts are ready to pray, and then trust the Holy Spirit to use that preparation and to give them the right words to say at the right time and in the right way. Studied extemporaneous prayer helps leaders to pray with simpler language and to come from the heart when they do so. It also cultivates a dependence upon the Lord for the words to say and the passion with which to say them.

Does prayer involve listening to God?

The idea of listening to God when we pray needs to be carefully qualified. There are passages of Scripture that suggest that God speaks to us when we pray. The back-and-forth between Abraham and the Lord in Genesis 18:22–33 points in this direction. David routinely speaks of being silent before the Lord and hearing the Lord answer his prayer (see Pss. 6:1–2, 9–10; 51:8; 62:1, 5, 11–12; 143:1, 8). Habakkuk, too, seems to hear the Lord responding in the midst of his prayer (see Hab. 3:16). And the same can be said about Jesus and Paul in the New Testament as well (see John 12:28; 2 Cor. 12:8–9).

In all these cases, however, we should be very careful about making a one-to-one correspondence between these individuals' experiences and our own. Each of these figures occupied a unique office and fulfilled a particular function in redemptive history. We may be called to be like Christ in our Christian lives, but we shouldn't expect that everything that happened to Jesus will also happen to us. And the same can be said of Moses, David, Habakkuk, and Paul. Just because they heard God speak doesn't mean that we will in the same way.

What is more, Scripture is our final word from God. Whereas God spoke in the past "at many times and in many ways," the person, work, and teaching of Jesus has brought an end to God's revelatory work (Heb. 1:1–2). With the closing of the final book of the New Testament, the book of Revelation, there is nothing else to be said—nothing to be added or taken away (see Rev. 22:18–19)—because the Bible, as we have it, is sufficient for faith and the Christian life (see Ps. 119:105; 2 Tim. 3:16).

This means that we ought not to expect God to speak to us in prayer in a revelatory fashion. We ought not to look for new (or extrabiblical) revelation from him, because he has already given us his final word in and through Jesus Christ. So listening for God to speak to us in prayer entails waiting for him to call things to our minds. It may be Bible verses that the Holy Spirit brings to the forefronts of our minds to address our current situations. It may be an idea that suddenly occurs to us that we never thought of before. I have personally experienced this quite frequently as a pastor when praying during sermon preparation. Often in a moment of silence in prayer, a specific idea or application will come to my mind that I hadn't previously thought about.

Martin Luther admitted that when he prayed the Lord's Prayer, he often lost himself in thought, meditating on one particular petition so extensively that he forgot to pray the rest of them. He then urged his readers, if this kind of thing ever happened to them, to "disregard" everything else, "listen in silence, and under no circumstances obstruct" the thoughts that come to mind, because it is at that moment that the Holy Spirit is "preach[ing]" to them. Luther encouraged his readers to "be still and listen to him" and to write everything down, because "one word of his sermon is far better than a thousand of our prayers." Luther even went so far as to say, "Many times I have learned more from one prayer than I might have learned from much reading and speculation."[6]

The thoughts or ideas that we take away from the Holy Spirit's "preaching" need to be held up to the light of Scripture. We shouldn't take them blindly as being definitively from the Lord. For all we know, we may be "hearing" last night's pizza, or we may even be hearing Satan, who masquerades as "an angel of light" (2 Cor. 11:14). God will never "preach" to us in any way that is contradictory to his revealed will in the Bible. He is the same yesterday, today, and forevermore (see Heb. 13:8). He is immutable and does not change his mind. He is truth, and he always speaks the truth. Satan, however, is "a liar and the father of lies" (John 8:44).

The dialogical give-and-take dynamic of relationships in general leads us to expect that God will speak to us in prayer. Prayer is not a one-way unloading of our wants and desires onto the Lord. It is two-way intimacy. To borrow the words of Samuel Rutherford again, not only does our faith "kiss" the Lord when we pray, but he "kisses" us as well. Prayer is a means of grace precisely because it is two-way intimacy.

If listening to God is appropriate, does that mean that contemplative prayer is too?

Depending on what we mean by contemplative prayer, it can be either good or bad. Typically, it is associated with Eastern and New Age religions, and in this sense, it involves a more mystical approach to prayer. It often encourages the use of breathing techniques and practices like "centering"—repeating a word or phrase over and over again to clear the mind. Even when it doesn't, its ultimate goal is generally to foster a feeling of oneness with the Lord. If this is what we mean by contemplative prayer, I would say that it is an unhelpful practice for Christians to engage in for several reasons.

First, this kind of contemplative prayer tends to downplay the traditional and biblical aspects of prayer—adoration, confession, thanksgiving, and supplication (ACTS)—in favor of a wordless and petition-less feeling of union and communion. But this runs counter to the Lord's explicit teaching on prayer in both Matthew 6 and Luke 11. In these passages, Jesus teaches his disciples to pray, and he unambiguously instructs them to use words and to make specific kinds of petitions. While words may be unnecessary on certain occasions for Christians, the general teaching of these two passages is that this should be the exception rather than the rule. If prayer is meant to be done contemplatively, then we would expect to see some sign of that in these passages. But instead we see the exact opposite.

Second, this kind of contemplative prayer tends to emphasize the loss of the individual within God or within the surrounding world. But the Bible does not portray prayer in this way either. Union and communion with God is an important part of Christian prayer, as we can see in so many of the Psalms, the example of Christ in the Gospels, and the way we have defined prayer according to Scripture in this book. But this union and communion never involves the loss of the individual. The lines between the individual, God, and the surrounding universe are never transgressed or blurred in prayer. The goal of prayer, according to the Scriptures, is not for us to be absorbed into God or into the world around us but for us to pour out our hearts to the Lord. In other words, prayer is our faith expressing itself to God, not us losing ourselves within the being of God.

Third, Christian prayer does not involve or seek after an emptying of the mind. Rather, in prayer our minds are fully engaged. Paul says as much in 1 Corinthians 14:15: "I will pray with my spirit, but I will pray with my mind also." The very definition of prayer as pleading also leads us in this direction. It is hard to conceive of pleading our case and emptying our minds at the same time.

Prayer as depicted in the Bible never involves clearing our minds, calming our psyches, and ridding ourselves of stress in order to feel God's presence or enjoy communion with him. Rather, we are told to cast all our burdens, cares, and stresses on the Lord in the very act of prayer and thereby to enjoy communion with him in and through that process (see Ps. 55:22; 1 Pet. 5:7). That is why Paul says, "Do not be anxious about anything, but in everything by prayer and supplication with thanksgiving let your requests be made known to God" (Phil. 4:6). In whatever life circumstances we find ourselves, we are to go to the Lord in prayer and cast our cares on him by making genuine "requests" of him. We are not to calm ourselves first by worldly techniques, however helpful they may otherwise be. The preparation that we rightly ought to do for prayer is not a calming of our souls or an emptying of our minds but rather a resting in the Lord and a filling of our minds with tangible reminders from Scripture of what we are doing and before whom we are going in prayer.

When the term "contemplative prayer" is used to describe the practice of listening to God, it refers to the dialogical nature of prayer as a two-way conversation. If this is what we mean by contemplative prayer, then the term is not so unhelpful. In fact, it can be perfectly appropriate (see the discussion above on listening to God in prayer). But because of the potential confusion regarding the term, it is probably better to speak of listening to God (or being silent in his presence) as a part of what we do in prayer rather than to speak of it as contemplative prayer.

Should Christians pray for the dead or for things that have already happened?

Most of us have had the experience of being asked to pray for something that will take place at a certain hour and then forgetting to do so until the hour is already past, so this question is a very practical one for us. If we forget to pray for someone who has a 10:00 a.m. appointment, can we still do so at 1:00 p.m.? What about the next day? And what about praying for people after they die?

In his book *Miracles,* C. S. Lewis argues that it is not wrong to pray for things that have already happened. He acknowledges that while it is true that the event in question has already been decided, it is also true that it has already been decided from before the foundation of the world. Thus, *every* prayer is prayed after the event or situation in question has been decided in the mind of God. If we pray at 11:00 a.m. or at 1:00 p.m. for a meeting that is supposed to take place at noon, we are, either way, praying after the outcome of that meeting has been decided. As long as we don't know the outcome ourselves, Lewis says we can rightly pray after the fact. But if we do know the outcome, we cannot legitimately pray, because to do so would be to reject the revealed will of God.[7]

Lewis's point is very helpful. All prayer takes place after the course of every event or circumstance has already been determined in the mind of God. And, as we have pointed out previously, God does not change, and he does not change his mind. Prayer does not bring him any information that he didn't already possess. It does not remind him of anything that he has forgotten. He knows all, and he remembers all. He has decreed what will come to pass, and not only is his decree unchangeably determined, but it is best. This decree remains hidden from us, however, until and unless it is revealed to us in the Bible or until and unless we see or experience it in time and space for ourselves. As long as neither of these things happens, we can legitimately pray. And God, who is not bound by time, can answer our prayers before we ever pray them.

But if we do know God's will—either because he has revealed it to us in his Word or because we have seen or experienced it for ourselves in time and space—we are never rightly to pray for a different outcome. To do so is to refuse to submit to God's will, which is rebellion and idolatry. In this sense, it would be wrong to pray for a different outcome to a lunch meeting after that meeting has already occurred and the outcome is known. It would also be wrong to pray for someone to be converted who has already died in an obviously unconverted state. But it would not necessarily be wrong to pray for a certain outcome to a lunch meeting that has already occurred if we do not know that outcome when we pray. And it would not necessarily be wrong to pray for someone to *have been* converted in life, before he or she died, if the state of that person's soul is unknown to us.

What can churches do to encourage Christians to pray together?

The single best thing churches can do to encourage Christians to pray together is to organize and conduct a regular weekly period of prayer. The "midweek prayer meeting" has fallen by the wayside in many twenty-first-century churches—and to our great detriment.

Here are a few thoughts to help us to reclaim this practice:

- *Pick a day and time that works best for people's schedules, and be flexible.* Wednesday nights may not be the best for this. But, then again, maybe they are. I recommend providing food and childcare. This makes it as easy as possible for busy families with young children to participate. Be willing to change the day and time as necessary to keep up with changes in people's schedules.
- *Consider using technology.* The use of videoconferencing technology allows those who cannot make the prayer meeting in person to participate virtually.
- *Lead by example.* Church members will never see the prayer meeting as important if the pastor(s) and leaders of the church do not see it as important. If leaders excuse themselves from the prayer meeting before the time of prayer, the rest of the people will get the message.
- *Put together prayer requests beforehand.* In typical prayer meetings, more time is spent in taking requests than in actually praying. Putting together prayer points beforehand allows more time to be spent in actual prayer and also ensures that the items being prayed for are kingdom focused. As proper as it is to pray for Johnny's upcoming

surgery, we need to ensure that we reserve some forum for prayers that are specifically focused on kingdom issues. We need to pray, "Thy kingdom come" and to do so with intentionality and vigor. I have personally used the Lord's Prayer as a guide to structure prayer meetings. By spending ten to fifteen minutes in each of four or five different areas—for instance, (1) "Our Father in heaven, hallowed be your name," (2) "Your kingdom come, your will be done, on earth as it is in heaven," (3) "Give us this day our daily bread," and (4) "forgive us our debts, as we also have forgiven our debtors" (Matt. 6:9–12)—we can ensure that we are not only praying kingdom prayers but also including adoration, confession, and supplication.

- *Consider using various forums.* Prayer meetings don't always have to be held in one large group. Why not break into smaller groups from time to time? This allows more people to pray for longer periods and removes the intimidation factor that many feel about praying in a larger setting. It may be that a combination of these forums would work best. Why not start in small groups and then come back together as a large group for the final few minutes together?
- *Consider asking leaders to be ready to pray short prayers during stretches of silence to keep things*

moving. Protracted periods of silence can be very discouraging. Having several leaders on standby to fill in the gaps will help to prevent this. Having them ready to pray short prayers will not intimidate the rest of the people and may encourage those who might not pray otherwise to pray a short prayer of their own.

- *Don't be discouraged by low attendance.* Keep pushing ahead. Look for opportunities to build the prayer awareness of the congregation by praying immediately for needs as they arise within the church. Don't just tell someone that you will pray for them; do it right then and there. In that way, you will build a culture of prayer within the congregation, and that will in turn impact the attendance at prayer meetings over time.
- *Pray specifically.* Christians tend to pray general prayers: "Please bless Bob" or "Please help Sally." Those are all fine, but who knows when the Lord has actually answered those prayers? What does "blessing" or "helping" look like in those situations? If we pray for specific requests, we know when a prayer has been answered. Then we can celebrate the answers we receive as publicly as we can. Seeing God answer prayer, in turn, encourages God's people to pray specifically and to participate in prayer meetings, too, which gives more opportunities to see God answer prayer, and so on.

Is it appropriate for Christians to pray to Mary or to the angels?

It is not appropriate for Christians to pray to Mary, to the angels, or to anyone other than God himself. The Lord is not only all-powerful but also all-wise and altogether good. Nothing in all the universe is more powerful than he is, and no one is wiser or better. He is working for our best interests through everything that comes into our lives (see Rom. 8:28). No one needs to plead our cause in his presence, and no one needs to incline him toward us. He is already as inclined to us as he could ever possibly be. We don't need Mary or the angels, or anyone else for that matter, to curry God's favor on our behalf. The death of the Lord Jesus on the cross has done that for us forevermore.

How should we pray for non-Christians?

The primary way that we should pray for non-Christians is to ask the Lord to bring them to faith in Jesus Christ. That should be our overriding concern. As sweet as the return of the Lord will be for Christians, it will be a far different thing for those who do not believe. On the last day, unbelievers will even go so far as to call upon the mountains to fall on them and shield them from the gaze of the Lord, so terrible will it be to them (see Isa. 2:10; Hos. 10:8; Luke 23:28–30; Rev. 6:16–17). If we genuinely want what is best for non-Christians, we will pray that they turn from their unbelief and place their hope and trust in Christ.

What about the "imprecatory" psalms? Do they allow us to pray for the destruction of our enemies?

The "imprecatory" psalms explicitly call for the destruction of the Lord's enemies—not in general but in particular. Thus in Psalm 58:6–11, David prays very specifically for the destruction of the enemies of the Lord who are persecuting him and who are standing against the Lord at that particular moment (see also Pss. 69:22–28; 109:6–20). Some people suggest that it is appropriate for Christians to follow the pattern of these psalms and to pray for the destruction of specific enemies of the Lord who exhibit an intractable hardness of heart and rebellion against the Lord and who array themselves against the Lord and his people in an oppressive manner or for a prolonged period of time. But I think we should be very careful with adopting these imprecations as our own.

The imprecatory psalms are typological. They point ahead to the last day—the day when God will finally destroy all his and our enemies and put to right every wrong that has ever been perpetrated against us. As we have indicated already, this day will be so harrowing for the enemies of the Lord that they will even call on the mountains to fall on them and hide them. The fact that the imprecatory psalms point ahead to the last day indicates that it would be improper for us to pray them in regard to specific individuals in specific circumstances in our lives, even if those individuals exhibit intractable hardness of heart and array themselves against the Lord and against us in oppressive or violent ways. For one thing, we don't know the mind of the Lord. God may be planning to bring such individuals to faith in Christ in the very near future. Those people could be modern-day versions of the apostle Paul. Would it be appropriate for us to pray for God to "pour out [his] indignation upon" such a person and "let [his] burning anger overtake" him or her, as David does in Psalm 69:24? If such a person is one of God's elect, then God has already poured out his indignation on Jesus for everything that person has ever done (even though it hasn't yet been applied to him or her by the Holy Spirit in time and space). I don't see how it would be appropriate to pray this, any more than it would be to pray for a specific person to be cursed (see Ps. 109:17–19) when Christ may well already have been made a curse in that person's place when he died on the cross.

For another thing, the Bible teaches us that God is sovereign even over the seasons of difficulty and pain in our lives and that he is using them for our good and for his own glory (see Ps. 115:1; Hab. 2:14; Rom. 8:28). It might be better for us, therefore, if these individuals are not destroyed or if God's "burning anger" doesn't overtake them just yet (Ps. 69:24). It might be better for us if our enemies are allowed to remain a thorn in our flesh for a while, because it might cause us to cast ourselves on the Lord and to trust him more. That was the case with Paul and his thorn in the flesh. Whatever that thorn may have been, it caused him to see that God's grace was sufficient and that God's power was "made perfect in weakness" (2 Cor. 12:9).

Having said this, however, I would say that it is appropriate for us to pray the imprecatory psalms in a *general* sense. It is appropriate for us to long to see "justice roll down like waters, and righteousness like an ever-flowing stream" (Amos 5:24) and to pray for these things to come to pass generally in God's timing and according to his purposes. It is appropriate for us to seek vindication from the Lord and to ask for him to make right all the wrongs that we have generally experienced—whatever that might look like—and, then, to wait patiently for God to do so at the proper time (see Rev. 6:9–11). It is fitting for us to pray for all who persistently resist God and stand against his work—generally speaking—to be judged and for God to be glorified in his ultimate triumph over all who oppose him.

And it is also appropriate for us to pray that God would restrain specific individuals and groups in specific circumstances, that he would bring specific injustices to an end, and that he would ultimately bring every individual who is living at enmity with the Lord and with the Lord's people to faith in Jesus Christ. It is also right for us to seek the help of civil authorities to restrain specific injustices and to put to right what is wrong (see Rom. 13:1–7), all the while praying for justice to be done and for all who do not believe in Christ to come to faith in him.

RECOMMENDED RESOURCES

Bounds, E. M. *Power Through Prayer*. Grand Rapids: Baker Book House, 1991. [This is a short, readable, convicting book calling Christians to devote themselves to prayer. Eric Alexander once told me that he read this book every year to remind him of the importance of prayer in his life and ministry.]

Carson, D. A. *A Call to Spiritual Reformation: Priorities from Paul and His Prayers*. Grand Rapids: Baker Book House, 1992. [Carson provides a survey of the apostle Paul's prayers and draws lessons from them in order to strengthen our prayer lives and grow us as pray-ers.]

Henry, Matthew. *A Method for Prayer*. Edited by J. Ligon Duncan III. Ross-shire, UK: Christian Focus Publications, 1994. [Henry's book is a helpful how-to guide on prayer. Henry surveys the Scriptures and uses the language of the Bible to help to teach us prayers of adoration, confession, thanksgiving, supplication, and intercession.]

Kelly, Douglas F. *If God Already Knows, Why Pray?* Ross-shire, UK: Christian Focus Publications, 1995. [Kelly walks us through the sovereignty of God and how that applies to prayer. He also encourages us to pray by addressing some of the issues that keep us from praying. This is a very helpful and encouraging read with many insightful illustrations and stories from Kelly's experiences around the world.]

Miller, Samuel. *Thoughts on Public Prayer*. Harrisonburg, VA: Sprinkle Publications, 1985. [This is the most helpful work I know of on praying in public. Miller deals with frequently asked questions and then unpacks several of the most common faults in public prayer, together with a description of what good public prayer looks like and how we can get to that point in our own lives and ministries.]

Ryle, J. C. "Prayer." In Practical Religion: Being Plain Papers on the Daily Duties, Experience, Dangers, and Privileges of Professing Christians, 63–96. Edinburgh: Banner of Truth Trust, 1998. [Ryle delivers a convicting chapter that encourages us to pray by focusing on the necessity of prayer. He especially emphasizes prayer as spiritual breathing. This chapter is eminently readable, very convicting, and well worth the time you spend in it.]

NOTES

Foreword

1 David E. Garland, *1 Corinthians*, Baker Exegetical Commentary on the New Testament (Grand Rapids: Baker Academic, 2003), 674.

Introduction: The Blessing of Prayer

1 Joseph Scriven, "What a Friend We Have in Jesus," 1855.

Chapter 1: The Nature of Prayer

1 Westminster Shorter Catechism, answer 98. See also Westminster Larger Catechism, answer 178, which defines prayer as "an offering up of our desires unto God, in the name of Christ, by the help of his Spirit; with confession of our sins, and thankful acknowledgement of his mercies." The only difference between the two is that the Larger Catechism includes one short phrase (six words) that the Shorter Catechism does not—"by the help of his Spirit"—and the Shorter Catechism includes one short phrase (six words) that the Larger Catechism does not—"for things agreeable to his will."

2 See *Westminster Confession of Faith* (Glasgow: Free Presbyterian Publications, 1995), 268, 315. Other more recent editions of the catechisms, like that published by the Orthodox Presbyterian Church, for instance, have included extra Scripture proof texts above and beyond the original one. See *The Confession of Faith and Catechisms: The Westminster Confession of Faith and Catechisms as Adopted by the Orthodox Presbyterian Church with Proof Texts* (Willow Grove, PA:

Committee on Christian Education, 2005), 333, 400, which adds Psalm 10:17 and Matthew 7:7–8 to the original.

3 John Bunyan defines prayer as a "pouring out of the heart or soul to God" and then goes on to speak of it in terms of pleading. See "A Discourse Touching Prayer," in *The Works of John Bunyan*, ed. George Offor (Edinburgh: Banner of Truth, 1991), 1:623–40. Charles Spurgeon, too, believed that prayer was essentially pleading: "Do not reckon you have prayed unless you have pleaded, for pleading is the very marrow of prayer." Charles Spurgeon, "Pleading" (sermon on Psalm 70:5, Metropolitan Tabernacle, London, October 28, 1871). Available at https://www.spurgeon.org/resource-library/sermons/ pleading/#flipbook/.

4 See Luke 5:12; 8:28, 38; 9:38, 40; Acts 21:39; 26:3; 2 Cor. 5:20; 8:4; 10:2; and Gal. 4:12.

5 As Alfred Edersheim has demonstrated, the Jewish people of old were always known for their hospitality. From their earliest years, Jewish citizens were taught not to consider their homes and belongings as their own but to "let thy house be wide open" to guests. See Alfred Edersheim, *Sketches of Jewish Social Life* (Peabody, MA: Hendrickson Publishers, 1994), 46–49.

6 Samuel Rutherford, *Letters of Samuel Rutherford*, ed. Andrew A. Bonar (Edinburgh, 1891), 71.

7 Richard Baxter, *The Reformed Pastor*, ed. William Brown (Edinburgh: Banner of Truth Trust, 1974), 61–63.

8 This phrase was apparently used by Johannes Kepler in the sixteenth century but became a staple within Reformed circles through the writing of men like Herman Bavinck and Cornelius Van Til. See Herman Bavinck, *Reformed Dogmatics*, vol. 1, ed. John Bolt, trans. John Vriend (Grand Rapids: Baker Academic, 2003), 44, and Cornelius Van Til, *A Christian Theory of Knowledge* (Nutley, NJ: Presbyterian and Reformed, 1969), 16.

Chapter 2: Prayer Works

1 See "Mega Millions," Lottery USA, last modified June 22, 2021, https://www.lotteryusa.com/mega-millions/.

2 I wrote about the name Israel and its significance for God's people in an article for *Tabletalk*. See Guy M. Richard, "Our Blessed Struggle," *Tabletalk*, December 2009, 64. Available at https://tabletalkmagazine.com/article/2009/12/our-blessed-struggle/.

3 See Acts 7:45 and Hebrews 4:8, both of which are clearly talking about the Old Testament patriarch Joshua. The Greek name used on both occasions is *Jesus*.

4 This is not intended to be a comprehensive list of passages. In addition to the verses cited in the main body of text, see also Prov. 15:8; Isa. 59:1–2; Jer. 7:16–17; 11:11–12; and 1 John 3:22.

5 Fanny J. Crosby, "Pass Me Not, O Gentle Savior," 1868.

6 Joni Eareckson Tada, "A Bruised Reed" (lecture, 2000 Ligonier National Conference, Orlando, FL). Available at https://www.ligonier.org/learn/conferences/holiness_00_national/a-bruised-reed/.

7 Thus, Sinclair Ferguson says, "Even if one were to grant what is sometimes too readily assumed—that healing is much more frequent among continuationists [those who see the extraordinary gifts of the Holy Spirit as continuing] than among cessationists [those who see them as ceasing with the close of the apostolic age]—the reason may not lie in the interpretive grid adopted but in the faith which seeks (and may even anticipate) the intervention of God." See Sinclair B. Ferguson, *The Holy Spirit* (Downers Grove, IL: InterVarsity Press, 1996), 236.

8 C. H. Spurgeon, "Opening the Mouth," in *C. H. Spurgeon's Sermons on Prayer*, ed. Charles T. Cook (London: Marshall, Morgan & Scott, 1959), 93.

Chapter 3: Prayer Is Necessary

1 John Calvin, *Institutes of the Christian Religion*, ed. John T. McNeill, trans. Ford Lewis Battles (Philadelphia: Westminster Press, 1960), 1.6.1 and 1.14.1.

2 J. C. Ryle, *Practical Religion: Being Plain Papers on the Daily Duties, Experience, Dangers, and Privileges of Professing Christians* (Edinburgh: Banner of Truth Trust, 1998), 64.

3 Ryle, 65.

4 For more on this, see my discussion on the relational nature of

saving faith in Guy M. Richard, *What Is Faith?* (Phillipsburg, NJ: P&R Publishing, 2012), 10–15.

5 See Calvin, *Institutes,* 3.1.3. See also Samuel Rutherford's use of Martin Luther in *A Survey of the Spirituall AntiChrist* (London, 1648), 126. Rutherford cites Luther in Latin with approval and then translates him into English.

6 Samuel Rutherford, *A Sermon Preached before the Honourable House of Lords* (London, 1645), 50.

7 Samuel Rutherford, *The Covenant of Life Opened* (Edinburgh, 1654), 351, with spelling updated.

8 John Piper, "Prayer: The Work of Missions" (lecture, ACMC Annual Meeting, Denver, CO, July 29, 1988). Available at https://www.desiringgod.org/messages/prayer-the-work-of-missions.

Chapter 4: Growing in Prayer

1 C. S. Lewis, *The Lion, the Witch and the Wardrobe* (1950; New York: Collier Books, 1970), 64.

2 James Montgomery Boice, *Christ's Call to Discipleship* (1986; Grand Rapids: Kregel Publications, 1998), 10.

Questions and Answers on Prayer

1 Westminster Shorter Catechism, answer 6.

2 John Bunyan, "A Discourse Touching Prayer," in *The Works of John Bunyan,* ed. George Offor (Edinburgh: Banner of Truth, 1991), 1:635.

3 Richard B. Gaffin, Jr., *Perspectives on Pentecost: New Testament Teaching on the Gifts of the Holy Spirit* (Phillipsburg, NJ: Presbyterian and Reformed, 1979), 84.

4 Gaffin, 84.

5 The answer to the three questions about fasting are drawn from an article that I wrote for *Tabletalk.* See Guy M. Richard, "Should Christians Fast?" *Tabletalk* (blog), November 9, 2018, https://tabletalkmagazine.com/posts/should-christians-fast/.

6 Martin Luther, "A Simple Way to Pray," in *Luther's Works,* vol. 43, ed. Gustav K. Wiencke (Philadelphia: Fortress Press, 1968), 198, 201–2.

7 C. S. Lewis, *Miracles: A Preliminary Study* (London: Geoffrey Bles, 1948), 214–15.